ACRL Publications in Librarianship no. 50

Academic Library Centrality: User Success through Service, Access, and Tradition

Deborah J. Grimes

Association of College and Research Libraries
a division of the American Library Association
Chicago 1998

The paper used in this publication meets the minimum requirements of American National Standard for Information Sciences–Permanence of Paper for Printed Library Materials, ANSI Z39.48—1992.∞

Library of Congress Cataloging-in-Publication Data
Grimes, Deborah J.
  Academic library centrality : user success through service, access, and tradition / Deborah J. Grimes.
      p.   cm. -- (ACRL publications in librarianship ; no. 50)
  Includes bibliographical references.
  ISBN 0-8389-7950-5 (alk. paper)
    1. Academic libraries--United States--Administration.
  2. Universities and colleges--United States--Administration.
  I. Title. II. Series.
  Z674.A75 no. 50
  [Z675.U5]
  025.1'977--dc21   98-19628

Printed in the United States of America.

02 01 00 99 98   5 4 3 2 1

Table of Contents

1. An Old Metaphor and a New Concept   1

2. Centrality in Organization Theory   23

3. A Study of Academic Library Centrality   56

4. What University Administrators Say about Centrality   71

5. User Success Through Service, Access, and Tradition   95

Appendix A. Interview Questions   126

Appendix B. Descriptions of Empirical Indicators of Academic Library Centrality   130

Bibliography   138

Index   150

With thanks to Steve Wiberley for his
painstaking editorial assistance
and to my family for their
never-ending support.

1. An Old Metaphor and a New Concept

The library is the heart of the university—or the college—or the school. Leaders in higher education and academic librarians have used this metaphor regularly for more than one hundred years. Although not precise, the metaphor implies primacy for the library. But in the practice of academic librarianship, we have seen something different. We have seen the distance between teaching and the library, first identified fifty years ago, at best remain the same and at worst widen. This gap is reflected in national educational initiatives that mention libraries, if at all, only in passing. It is demonstrated by professors who do not integrate the library into their instruction, characterized by little more than study hall use of libraries by students, and marked by faculty and administrators' misperceptions of the librarians' potential in instruction. We have seen budget allocations for library services and resources, in general, diminish. Such budgetary limitations particularly affect periodicals subscriptions, staffing, and services for students and faculty. We have also seen planning for technology take place on campuses without significant involvement of librarians, and we have seen organizational structures emerge in which the library director or dean no longer participates in decision-making at the highest levels of university administration. Finally, we have seen some librarians clinging to the "heart of the university" metaphor, assuming that the relationships it implies are

1

what libraries *should* be and bemoaning the lack of insight by university administrators and faculty. Being at the heart of university life implies that there is no gap between instruction and the library, that funding for the library is protected, and that the university organization recognizes a legitimate role for librarians, especially library directors, in campus decision-making.

This is not to say that academic libraries are doomed. On the contrary, much good work is accomplished in academic libraries today. The resources they provide to students and faculty are more varied than ever before, and new services are being developed every day. On some campuses, the library and its staff play a significant role in the education of students. In general, however, there is a tension between what many librarians *think* the library is—the heart of the university—and what is seen on campuses today. By accepting the "heart of the university" metaphor, many librarians cling to the implied organizational relationships. Willie L. Parson suggests that acceptance of the metaphor influences librarians' interactions with the university community. It creates "self-justifying and self-limiting beliefs about the practices of [librarians], organization of the library, and the institutional identity of the library."[1]

Although there are serious problems with continuing to use the "heart of the university" metaphor, we must realize that, to some extent, it can be equated with *centrality*, a key concept in current academic librarianship and in analysis of higher education. The 1989 "Standards for University Libraries: Evaluation of Performance" identifies centrality as an underlying assumption that governs the effectiveness of the academic library within the university:

> The library is of *central* importance to the institution. It is an organic combination of people, collections, and buildings, whose purpose is to assist users in the process of transforming information into knowledge.
>
> Information and knowledge are *central* to the attainment of any university's goals. The ways in which information is collected, stored, and distributed within the institution will, in large measure, determine the level and success of scholarship and research.[2]

Like the "heart of the university" metaphor, the standards' use of the term *central* points to the fact that libraries are fundamental to any academic institution. Unlike the "heart of the university" metaphor, centrality in the standards points to some definite, albeit broad, things the library should do (assist users; collect, store, and distribute information). But standing by itself, undeveloped, the term *centrality* does not tell librarians enough. Fortunately, the concept of centrality has been key in helping academicians understand how an academic department contributes to the university's mission and, subsequently, how it accrues the power necessary to acquire resources that support its programs and activities. Using research methods similar to those used to study the centrality of academic departments, librarians can begin to understand better the ways in which academic libraries are central to the needs of the university. The purpose of this book is to report the findings of one study of the centrality of the academic library and to suggest specific ways in which the library can fulfill its mission. This book aims to improve librarians' understanding of how to help their users succeed and seeks a new metaphor for the academic library that is appropriate for the turn of the century. More important, this book provides evidence of what leaders in academia really expect of libraries and librarians.

The "Heart of the University" Metaphor

Because of its past power and current weakness, the "heart of the university" metaphor bears close scrutiny. We can begin our examination with a brief look at the development of higher education and librarianship in the United States, which provided the context in which the metaphor originated. The American research library emerged in the late 1800s in an era of significant change in American higher education and librarianship. These changes were launched by the Morrill Acts of 1861 and 1890 and the Hatch Act of 1887, which expanded higher education in the United States and changed the content and emphasis of the college curriculum. The growth of industrialization following the Civil War also influenced the curriculum, moving it from classical studies to more applied scientific and technical studies.[3] Although Harvard University was the first to conform its professional schools to the "university ideal,"[4] Johns Hopkins University, founded in 1873, was the first in the United States to follow the German university model. It was the first American institution to stress research and to provide "a center of concentration, the association of other scholars, research materials, laboratories, and a means of publishing. Scholarship, rather than teaching, became the vital core . . . ."[5]

By setting the standard for research institutions during the late 1800s, Johns Hopkins University initiated a system of American universities.[6] Other institutions (e.g., Harvard, Cornell, Columbia) followed suit, influenced by scholars and administrators such as William Watts Fowler and James B. Angell. At the same time, university education moved from an elitist, privileged tradition of higher education toward a more egalitarian system.[7] According to Arthur T. Hamlin, these changes in higher education "created the need" for the American research library.[8]

In 1876, several events occurred that were significant to librarianship in the United States. The first was publication by the U. S. Bureau of Education of *Public Libraries in the United States: Their History, Condition, and Management.* This treatise emphasized for the first time the need for services based on the users' needs rather than on the needs of library management.[9] In a "complete about-face," librarians began to emphasize use of the library's collections rather than preservation. Hamlin cited this as the "single most important event in the history of the American academic library." Along with this fundamental change in the American view of library service came the founding of the American Library Association (ALA), providing librarians with an organization through which they could deal collectively and professionally with library issues and problems. Born in the same year, *Library Journal,* as a publication to distribute news, statistics, and articles on professional topics, gave librarians a formal voice. Another step for libraries was the establishment of Library Bureau as the first manufacturer of equipment and furniture designed specifically for library use. Finally, publication of Charles Ammi Cutter's *Rules for a Printed Catalog* (as Part II of the U.S. Bureau of Education report)[10] gave libraries a universal typology for recorded knowledge and an organizational scheme that standardized library practice throughout the country.[11]

It was in this context of change in librarianship and higher education in the late nineteenth century that the metaphor "the library is the heart of the university" came into vogue.[12] The metaphor was first used by Harvard University President Charles William Eliot, who served from

1869 to 1909.[13] Since then, the metaphor and its variations have dotted the landscape of published literature, conference speeches, and public discussion in both the professional and lay communities. In 1940, for example, Peyton Hurt observed:

> . . . wise administration should call for frequent study and analy-
> sis of college library functions, to give greater vitality to that
> often avowed "heart of the college."[14]

Later, Paul H. Buck[15] and Logan Wilson claimed "that the library is the heart of education."[16] Recently, in a point–counterpoint exchange in *College & Research Libraries News*, Frank R. Allen and Sarah Barbara Watstein debated the need to "promote the library as the heart of [the] campus."[17] Even library iconoclasts Walt Crawford and Michael Gorman have alluded to the metaphor in *Future Libraries: Dreams, Madness & Reality*:

> The library will . . . stand in the future as in the past as the
> heart of every good university, college and school . . . .[18]

As Richard M. Dougherty and Ann P. Dougherty have pointed out, however, some academic library administrators see discrepancies between the well-worn metaphor and reality:

> Pamela Snelson argued that it's time to shatter the myth of the
> library as "heart of the university" and to instead demonstrate
> specific ways libraries contribute to the institutional mission.[19]

A careful examination of the metaphor shows that critics are right. Whereas Hurt, Buck, and Logan linked the use of academic libraries with learning itself, other writers used the metaphor to reflect the symbolic value of the library on campus. Allen and Watstein referred to both the virtual and physical library, whereas Crawford and Gorman focused less on the technologies in use than on the fundamental services provided by the library. The metaphor seems most frequently to imply that the academic library should be important on campus and that it should be a central institutional resource—but it goes no further than that. Because people have used the "heart of the university" metaphor in so many ways, it has no power to inform the practice of academic librarianship. We must ask whether its continued use benefits libraries in any way.

The persistence of the "heart of the university" metaphor for more than one hundred years suggests that librarians and their academic colleagues make some fundamental assumptions about the relationship of the academic library to the university. These assumptions reflect the use of metaphor to define and describe social situations. In sociological theory, metaphors illustrate and describe social situations "from the viewpoint of something else."[20] We frequently see social metaphors used to describe organizations. For example, organizations have been characterized as anarchies, space stations, marketplaces, garbage cans, and as fairy tale characters such as Rumpelstiltskin.[21] Because metaphors are important in the description and study of organizational relationships, it is important to consider the authenticity of the "heart of the university" metaphor in viewing the relationship between the academic library and its institution.

Richard H. Brown proposed four criteria for evaluating a metaphor for sociological use: isomorphism, cogency, economy, and range. Although the "heart of the university" metaphor is certainly cogent, it is not economical. Focusing on *heart*, the key word in the metaphor, illustrates this point. There are, for instance, no fewer than fifty-six usages of the word *heart* cited in the *Oxford English Dictionary*.[22] Beyond the obvious physical comparisons of the "heart" of the institution to the heart of the body, other images evoked include: centrality of location, source of sentiment or emotion, source of life and nourishment, and source of spirituality and courage. This wealth of images—and ambiguities—provides neither librarians nor academics with a lens through which to clearly view the function of the library within the university. There are far too many images for isomorphic or one-to-one comparisons of form, and it is difficult to limit the range of comparisons for further exploration. We find, then, that "the library is the heart of the university" metaphor lacks precision and is of limited value in the formal study of academic librarianship. As a profession criticized for its lack of theory, librarianship cannot hold fast to metaphors (i.e., models) that are not useful conceptualizations of the real relationships between the academic library and the university. If models are stepping stones in the development of theory,[23] it is no wonder that librarianship has been slow to develop its own theories—it is trapped, as suggested by Parson, in self-limiting conceptualizations.[24] There are consequences for failing to more closely examine the "heart of the university" metaphor. Library educators may pass along misconceptions to their students, and academic library practitioners may fail to recognize actual organizational relationships. Lack of understanding, for example, makes it difficult for library administrators to negotiate effectively within the university for sufficient funding, to move beyond sentimental stereotypes that negatively influence the role of the library on campus, or to identify new areas in which library programs are needed.

Although a historical review and a sociological analysis of the "heart of the university" metaphor are very revealing, to truly appreciate the metaphor's current place, we need to look carefully at what it implies and what we find in the practice of librarianship. The following sections examine three major areas: the gap between instruction and the academic library; diminishing funding for academic libraries; and decision-making and organizational structure in today's universities.

The Gap between Instruction and the Academic Library

There is a gap between university instruction and the academic library. Fifteen years ago, *A Nation at Risk*, a national initiative for education reform, was published.[25] The omission of libraries from this report stunned the library community. To reassert the library's various roles in the educational process, librarians responded with several publications: *Alliance for Excellence: Librarians Respond to 'A Nation at Risk'*;[26] *Involvement in Learning: Realizing the Potential of American Higher Education*;[27] and *Integrity in the College Curriculum: A Report to the Academic Community*.[28] Despite these efforts, eight years later, *America 2000: An Education Strategy*,[29] the latest federal plan for higher education, mentioned libraries only once, in passing. Recently, the development of the National Information Infrastructure (NII) and the federal manifesto for information policy in the United States hold great promise for libraries. This promise is marred, however, by suggestions that the NII will render libraries and librarians obsolete. If libraries are indeed the heart of the university, we might expect to see academic libraries and librarians playing important roles in national educational initiatives such as these. We also might expect to find them playing more important roles in university classrooms.

Ernest L. Boyer, author of a Carnegie Foundation Study entitled *College: The Undergraduate Experience in America*, found that the library is a "neglected" resource, little used by faculty and students alike. Instead, "textbooks dominate the teaching and only occasionally [is] the library mentioned."[30] Most students use the library as a study hall, and one-half of the undergraduates in Boyer's survey spent no more than two hours per week in the library. Boyer concluded that the "gap between instruction and the library, reported almost half a century ago, still exists." Larry L. Hardesty also reported on this gap, citing several studies that show that the academic library serves chiefly as a study hall and reserve book room.[31] These reports suggest that academic libraries are not at the heart of the institution and its activities.

Contributing to this gap between instruction and the library are faculty views of the roles played by librarians within the university. In general, librarians are distanced from the educational endeavor and their participation in education is circumscribed by faculty perceptions. University president Gresham Riley, for instance, asserted that "most academic faculty are *not* predisposed to recognize and acknowledge a legitimate educational role for libraries and for librarians."[32] Librarian William A. Moffett frankly stated:

> We know that we have a vital role to play in higher education, but sometimes we become acutely aware that our colleagues have a remarkably superficial notion of who we are and what it is that we do.[33]

Studies of faculty perceptions of academic librarians support these observations. Almost twenty years after ACRL launched its campaign for faculty status, college and university faculty remain confused about librarians' roles in higher education.[34] For example, over one-third of the faculty in a university survey responded that the librarian's role in educating students is "very little" or "none."[35] Bill Crowley summed up the situation quite well:

Regardless of what academic librarians know about their actual value to faculty and administrators, the literature of higher education consistently portrays librarians as ancillary to the academic enterprise.[36]

In fact, librarians themselves remain divided and apparently confused over their place in the educational system.[37] "Faculty status," for instance, means different things at different institutions, and librarians at many institutions are reexamining faculty status and opting for different designations, such as "academic" or "academic professional" status. Responses provoked by "Faculty Status: 2001," a review of the issue sponsored by ACRL, offer "ample proof that this topic is still being hotly debated."[38] Being at the heart of university goals, however, implies that both faculty and librarians would have a clearer view of the librarian's role in education and would perceive the librarian to be a vital part of the educational process.

At the same time, the emergence of bibliographic instruction (BI) as a distinct professional discipline reflects an instructional commitment by librarians. Francis Hopkins pointed out that BI has more in common with an academic discipline than with the traditional practice of librarianship.[39] Michael Keresztesi compared the growth of the bibliographic instruction movement to the evolution of scientific disciplines.[40] However, these characteristics of the BI movement, not typical of librarianship, illustrate how far the library has grown from traditional university instruction. In fact, Trudi E. Jacobson and John R. Vallely suggested that librarians have not been successful in "forging partnerships" with other teaching colleagues. They stated:

> Despite the fact that bibliographic instruction has transformed and reshaped the manner in which college and university reference staffs define their role, and notwithstanding the substantial number of students and classroom teachers involved in BI programs, our teaching faculty colleagues have not, as a group, integrated BI into the body of material they feel it is essential to have students learn.[41]

Furthermore, academic librarians continue to debate the content and emphasis of bibliographic instruction. Parson, for example, said that critical thinking must be the priority that allows librarians to "legitimately speak of [the library's] centrality to the academic environment."[42] There remains a significant gap between instruction and the academic library, despite our assumption that libraries are the heart of the university.

Diminishing Funding for Academic Libraries

Other evidence that the academic library is not the heart of the university is in funding. Libraries once enjoyed protected status in university budgets. But since the 1960s, university financial officers have been unsympathetic to fiscal needs of academic libraries, using the well-known epithet "bottomless pit" when referring to the library's budgetary requirements.[43] More recently, Boyer found that "budget cuts often hit the library first" and that "only about one-half of all four-year college libraries in the country" meet the minimum ALA standards for annual expenditures.[44] Anne Woodsworth reflected that "competition for funds . . . [on university campuses] has intensified to the point that what was once a universal good (the library) is now perceived as just one more support service that must cost less and 'produce' more . . . ." [45]

Protected status is disappearing, and faculty often view the library's diminishing financial prospects as "someone else's problem."[46] In *The Economics of Research Libraries*, a study conducted for the Council on Library Resources (CLR), Martin M. Cummings reported that the financial commitment to the academic library is less today than thirty years ago.[47] Unfortunately, these budgetary decisions are based on the importance of the library to the university's image and standing in the academic community. A 1992 study of twenty-four members of the Association of Research Libraries (ARL) for the Andrew W. Mellon Foundation confirmed these observations: "rather than continuing to claim a larger and larger percentage of the university budget, the typical research library has seen its share of all [education and general (E&G)] expenditures fall steadily in recent years." Between the years 1960 and 1971, library budgets grew from less than three percent to almost four percent of the total E&G expenditures; however, research library budgets in 1990 bottomed out at 3.08 percent, just slightly higher than the budgets of the 1960s.[48] This is a particularly disheartening situation when viewed within the economic realities of increasing publication costs, especially those of essential research journals, and of costs associated with information technologies, consortia memberships, and networking. Librarians find themselves forced to choose between print and electronic resources when both are needed in academic libraries. In addition, financial problems have forced librarians to seek outside funding through development programs, which have become commonplace in academic libraries. Contrary to the philosophy of free library services, a growing number of academic libraries are instituting fee-based services to cover costs, especially of database use and document delivery. Costs associated with the NII and access to Internet and the World Wide Web also have implications for the provision of free access to information. The "universal good" of information, historically rooted in a democratic society and a system of public education, may be limited to those students and academic units that can afford to buy it. University budgets do not reflect a financial commitment to the library commensurate with its being the heart of the university.

Campus Decision-Making and Organizational Structures

The final evidence to suggest that academic libraries do not necessarily lie at the heart of universities is twofold: Specifically, librarians do not play significant roles in campus decisions on information technology; and, in general, library deans and directors do not participate in university administration at the highest levels.

In 1985, Allen B. Veaner predicted that the academic library will not remain a "campus monopoly, the Ma Bell of academe."[49] He warned that new information and telecommunications technologies are capable of changing important campus relationships. Veaner's prediction has come true, with computer centers or individual departments on some campuses supporting access to scholarly databases and other information sources. A study by Kenneth E. Flower for the ARL, for instance, showed that academic librarians in the 1980s had limited involvement on information policy committees and were not playing significant roles in campus-wide decisions about information policy. Flower concluded that academic libraries were not "a sphere of influence."[50] Almost ten years later, John Perry and Anne Woodsworth suggested that "libraries are seldom seen as leaders or even partners in campus-based innovations [including those involving new technologies], even those that touch at the core of their own operations—information services on campus."[51] Nancy Allen and James F. Williams III further observed that many senior administrators in libraries may not know very much about information technology and information policy."[52] Beginning in the late 1980s, a trend has developed in which the chief offices of the library and the computing center are combined under the administration of a chief information officer (CIO). Studies indicated that "by the end of 1989, one-third of higher education institutions in the nation either had or were searching for a Chief Information Officer."[53] Additional increases were predicted for the near future. This new organizational structure, however, does not mean that the library dean or director will rise to the position of "information 'czar'," as the CIO position has been called.[54] As a result, it is possible that the library may assume a more subordinate position within the university hierarchy.

Technology decisions are not the only ones to which librarians make limited contributions; other changes in university organizational structures are also affecting the academic library. More than twenty years ago, Arthur M. McAnally and Robert B. Downs reported in "The Changing Roles of Directors of University Libraries" that layers of university administration have been imposed between the library and the university's highest office. The effects of this layering of university administration have been to limit the library administrator's access to the institution's chief executive officer (CEO) and, in some cases, to the decision-making forum at the level of the vice president. The consequences, conclude McAnally and Downs, have been that the library director is no longer able to "get to the point of a showdown much less win one."[55] Fifteen years later, Woodsworth suggested that this trend continues, that "nothing has appeared to ameliorate the impact of removing easy access of the library director to the center of institutional power." In fact, she said that ". . . not only do diminishing opportunities for influencing decisions remain but there are even more new senior positions in universities that impose both demands and constraints on [academic library directors]."[56]

In the classic article, "The Bottomless Pit, or the Academic Library As Viewed from the Administration Building," Robert F. Munn reported that academic library directors of the 1960s knew little about the university as an organization.[57] Similarly, recent library researchers have found little focus in the literature on the broader university organization—despite the importance of the academic library's organizational relationships within the larger university structure.[58] Recent writers also lament the academic librarian's reactive rather than proactive stance, which may be explained in part by a lack of understanding of academia. Library and university administrators alike must recognize the need for the library director to grow stronger politically and to accept responsibility for a more active role on campus.[59] Herbert S. White, for example, affirmed that it is the responsibility of the academic library director "to help decide university priorities," calling for "greater involvement in the collegium of the university."[60]

Librarians and academics have observed the absence of major involvement by the academic library in the total organizational structure of the university and in its efforts to achieve institutional goals. In 1968, Munn reported that academic administrators "devote[d] little real thought to the library," exhibiting poor understanding and support of its role in higher education.[61] Larry Hardesty and David Kaser reassessed the situation in a study for the CLR, finding that the relationships have improved somewhat in college libraries.[62] Results of interviews with thirty-nine academic officers revealed that most college administrators are "reasonably well-informed about the service, operations, and contributions of academic libraries." Nevertheless, despite administrators' belief in the "important symbolic role" the library plays within the college, their "benign neglect" and lack of "real thought" first reported by Munn more than twenty years ago remains. Hardesty and Kaser found that contemporary library directors rarely participate in discussions of the institution's "inner circle." Although Hardesty and Kaser concluded that lack of feedback and familiarity "do not necessarily mean . . . lack of support," they maintained that there is certainly room for improvement. As members of a unit assumed to be the heart of the university, librarians and library administrators should be expected to play key roles in campus decision-making, whether for information technology, which directly affects their libraries, or for campus priorities in general. What we find, however, is that librarians and library administrators are often not as involved in the university's decision-making process as we expect them to be.

A New Starting Point

Having found the long-standing, ubiquitous metaphor "the library is the heart of the university" wanting, and in the process, having seen that the academic library's status, role, and fortune are far from what the metaphor implies, we need to seek a replacement for the metaphor and determine what the mission of the academic library should be. We need to do this because no organization can survive if it does not have a clear idea of what it is and what it should do. An organization's self-definition or self-description usually leads to a statement of what it should do—its mission. Although we have long had carefully crafted statements of the academic library's mission, we have not identified ways in which it contributes to the university's mission. The concept of centrality, used to identify the ways in which academic departments contribute to the university's mission, provides a starting point for answering the question: *How* can the academic library contribute substantially to the university?

To better understand centrality, we must examine organizational relationships within the university. We can use organization theory, which is defined by Pugh as "the systematic study of the structure, functioning, and performance of organizations and the behaviors of groups and individuals within them."[63] Because we want to know more about the "big picture," the "*macroperspective*"—the study of how and why an organization behaves as it does—holds the most promise for increasing our understanding of university–library relationships.[64] A review of the research on academic libraries reveals no consistent, successful application of organization theory to problems in librarianship.[65] Little research on library administration focuses on the academic library's external relationships. Leadership studies, which are numerous, often address the individual's influence on the library and its environment (or vice versa), but few studies address the larger roles of the library or its director within the university.[66] Helen A. Howard surmised that there is "an apparent lack of awareness and/or interest" among librarians in organization theory and its applications to libraries.[67] However, the most important decisions that affect the academic library's fate within the university—namely those regarding budget, curricula, and information technology—are made within the larger organizational context. These decisions are generally made not by librarians but by persons who have neither a direct role in the provision of library services nor in the resolution of library problems. As a result, study of the organizational views of university decision makers should be especially relevant to our understanding of library–university relationships.

There are at least two relevant bodies of organizational research that address university decision-making and the concept of centrality in academia. One is about retrenchment and the closing of academic departments or units within the university. The other deals with resource allocation and department power or influence, using the concept of centrality as a means of predicting resource allocation. Resource allocation is a concept that embodies both scarcity and choice—situations that most academic libraries will face well into the twenty-first century. Universities are operating with scarce financial resources and, as a result, are forced to choose how and if programs, departments, or services will be funded. Studies that address the rationale behind university financial and retrenchment choices are based on the assumption that all organizational units (e.g., departments, schools, offices, etc.) have resources that they contribute to the university's mission. These resources may include, for example, production of credit hours, prestige through national ranking or reputation, and service and administrative contributions to the university.[68] Increasingly, university choices are based in part on the centrality of a unit's resources or contributions to the university's mission.[69] Hanna Ashar and Jonathan Z. Shapiro have suggested that centrality is a major departmental characteristic taken into account by decision makers and that central departments survive better than peripheral ones in times of financial stress.[70]

Although several studies have identified measures or indicators of academic departmental centrality within the university, there are no research-based indicators of academic library centrality. The study reported in this book aimed to find such indicators by examining the centrality of the academic library within the general context of organization theory and within the specific contexts of resource allocation and retrenchment theory. Although it was *not* an attempt to validate or justify the role of the academic library in higher education or to assess the value of the library to the institution, it was a study of the individual activities, services, or resources of the academic library that support the mission of the university. The primary finding of the study is that there are several ways in which the academic library demonstrates its centrality to the university. These can be summed up in three categories: service, access, and tradition. The library's unique contributions to the mission of the university are focused on the success of library users. As such, academic library centrality is the degree to which the library promotes user success. The remainder of this book traces how we get to this definition of academic library centrality.

Summary

The phrase "the library is the heart of the university" emerged along with the American research library during the latter half of the nineteenth century. The metaphor implies that the academic library is of unparalleled importance. Despite its persistence for more than one hundred years, there is a considerable distance between the relationship it implies and institutional opinion and practice. Evidence of this difference is found in a number of areas. First, there is a gap between instruction and the academic library. Students and faculty alike fail to involve library resources and services in regular learning and instruction, turning to the library primarily as an undergraduate study hall or reserve book room. National initiatives to improve the quality of education in the United States fail to mention, much less to plan, improvement of library resources. Bibliographic instruction, growing as a separate academic discipline, remains on the periphery of college education despite the large numbers of students and librarians involved in BI on a regular basis. Related to this lack of library involvement in instruction is a lack of understanding of the potential role of the academic librarian. Faculty and administrators expect librarians to participate little, if any, in the education of students.

A second area of difference is a disheartening decrease in academic library share of institutional funding. This decrease is confirmed by Martin Cummings[71] for the CLR and by Anthony Cummings et al.[72] for the Andrew W. Mellon Foundation. This decrease has occurred despite dramatic increases in serials costs and costs associated with adoption of new information technologies and telecommunications. The decrease has led to a search for outside funding and the initiation of fee-based services.

Despite the need for academic librarians to be leaders and innovators with new campus information technologies, they remain, for the most part, on the periphery of decision-making and innovative processes. Some institutions are establishing the position of CIO (or similar title), but librarians are often not directly involved in information policy development. Other changes in the university organizational structure, including the addition of layers of administration, are altering the access of the library administrator to the center of institutional power. This is all the more significant for the academic library because many academic library directors fail to assume a proactive role within local campus politics. In all, the "library is the heart of the university" metaphor leads librarians and academics to erroneous conclusions about the real relationships between the library and the university. Librarians must move beyond the "heart of the university" metaphor and examine more closely actual organizational relationships. This examination is best done through the concept of centrality. Centrality is used by academic departments to determine the degree to which they contribute to the mission of the parent university; it is similar to the assumption of the 1989 ACRL "Standards for University Libraries" that "the library is of central importance to the institution" and that "information and knowledge are central to the attainment of any university's goals." Organization theory provides the basis for the study of centrality. Although there has been little effective application of organization theory to the study of the academic library's relationships with the university, there are two relevant bodies of organizational research—on retrenchment and resource allocation—that offer insight. More specifically, the study of resource allocation sheds light on departmental influence in institutional decision-making. The purpose of the study on which this book is based was to identify ways in which the academic library demonstrates centrality to the university mission.

This chapter has examined the "library is the heart of the university" metaphor and its shortcomings. It has outlined discrepancies between the metaphor and campus realities and identified centrality as a concept that offers much to the theory of academic librarianship. Chapter 2 traces key concepts related to centrality through the history of organization theory and through studies of retrenchment and resource allocation. It also looks closely at departmental or subunit power and its relationship to centrality. By examining existing theory, we will gain a better understanding of academic library centrality. Chapter 3, outlines the research methodology and research design used in the project on which this book is based. In addition, chapter 3 describes the seven universities and their leaders who participated in the study. Chapter 4 is very significant because it discusses the responses to interview questions of university CEOs and chief administrative officers (CAOs) at the seven institutions, with particular attention given to the examples they cited. These comments are evidence of what academic administrators think about libraries on university campuses. Finally, chapter 5 analyzes the findings of the study, developing both indicators and nonindicators of academic library centrality, some of which may be surprising. Implications of this analysis are outlined, along with suggestions for applying the findings to library practice. In the end, a new metaphor is proposed to replace the "heart of the university" metaphor and to use as a model that is more beneficial to both the theory and practice of academic librarianship.

Notes

1. Willie L. Parson, "User Perspective on a New Paradigm for Librarianship," *College & Research Libraries* 45 (Sept. 1984): 374–75.

2. ACRL, College Library Standards Committee, "Standards for University Libraries: Evaluation of Performance," *College & Research Libraries News* 30 (Sept. 1989): 679–91.

3. Arthur T. Hamlin, *The University Library in the United States: Its Origin and Development* (Philadelphia: Univ. of Pennsylvania Pr., 1981), 4–47.

4. Lee C. Deighton, ed. *Encyclopedia of Education* (New York: Macmillan and Free Pr., 1971), 343.

5. Hamlin, *The University Library in the United States*, 40–47.

6. Roger L. Geiger, *To Advance Knowledge: The Growth of American Research Universities, 1900–1940* (New York: Oxford Univ. Pr., 1986), 9.

7. Joseph Ben-David, *Centers of Learning: Britain, France, Germany, United States* (New York: McGraw-Hill, 1977), 24–28.

8. Hamlin, *The University Library in the United States*, 48.

9. U. S. Bureau of Education, *Public Libraries in the United States: Their History, Condition, and Management* (Washington, D.C.: Department of the Interior, 1876). Special Report.

10. Charles Ammi Cutter. *Rules for a Printed Dictionary Catalog* (Washington, D.C.: U.S. Bureau of Education, 1876).

11. Hamlin, *The University Library in the United States*, 22–46.

12. Ibid., 46.

13. Joanne R. Euster, "The Academic Library: Its Place and Role in the Institution," in *Academic Libraries: Their Rationale and Role in American Higher Education*, eds. Gerard R. McCabe and Ruth J. Person (Westport, Conn.: Greenwood Pr., 1995): 2.

14. Peyton Hurt, "Principles and Standards for Surveying a College Library," *College & Research Libraries* 11 (Mar. 1941): 110.

15. Paul H. Buck, *Libraries and Universities: Addresses and Reports* (Cambridge, Mass.: Belknap Pr. of Harvard Univ. Pr., 1964).

16. Logan Wilson, "Library Roles in American Higher Education," *College & Research Libraries* 31 (Mar. 1970): 99.

17. Frank R. Allen and Sarah Barbara Watstein, "Point/Counterpoint: The Value of Place," *College & Research Libraries News* 57 (June 1996): 373.

18. Walt Crawford and Michael Gorman, *Future Libraries: Dreams, Madness & Reality* (Chicago: ALA, 1995), 181.

19. Richard M. Dougherty and Ann P. Dougherty, "The Academic Library: A Time of Crisis, Change, and Opportunity," *Journal of Academic Librarianship* 18 (Jan. 1993): 343.

20. Richard H. Brown, *A Poetic for Sociology: Toward a Logic of Discovery for the Human Sciences* (Cambridge, England: Cambridge Univ. Pr., 1977): 77.

21. Karl E. Weick, *The Social Psychology of Organizations* (Reading, Mass.: Addison-Wesley, 1979), 47. Anarchies are used by Michael D. Cohen and James G. March, *Leadership and Ambiguity* (New York: McGraw-Hill, 1974); space stations by Karl E. Weick, "Organizational Design: Organizations as Self-Designing Systems," *Organizational Dynamics* 6 (autumn 1977): 30–46; marketplaces by P. Georgiou, "The Goal Paradigm and Notes toward a Counter Paradigm," *Administrative Science Quarterly* 18 (Sept. 1973): 291–310; garbage cans by Michael D. Cohen, James G. March, and Johan P. Olsen, "A Garbage Can Model of Organizational Choice," *Administrative Science Quarterly* (Mar. 1972): 1–25; Rumpelstiltskin by Kenwyn K. Smith and Valerie M. Simmons, "A Rumpelstiltskin Organization: Metaphors on Metaphors in Field Research," *Administrative Science Quarterly* 28 (Sept. 1983): 377–92. For further discussion of metaphorical devices in sociology, see Brown, *A Poetic for Sociology*, 77–171; John Lofland and Lyn H. Lofland, *Analyzing Social Settings: A Guide to Qualitative Observation and Analysis* (Belmont, Calif.: Wadsworth), 122–23.

22. *The Oxford English Dictionary*, 1989 ed. S.v. "Heart."

23. For a complete discussion of Brown's criteria for determining the adequacy of a metaphor for sociological use, see *A Poetic for Sociology*, 99–100. Brown suggests that metaphors are models (pp. 113–25). See also the discussion of metaphors and models in Lyndhurst Collins, *The Use of Models in Social Sciences* (Boulder, Colo.: Westview Pr., 1976), 16–43; Max Black, *Models and Metaphors: Studies in Language and Philosophy* (Ithaca, N.Y.: Cornell Univ. Pr., 1962), especially 219–43.

24. Parson, "User Perspective on a New Paradigm for Librarianship."

25. U.S. National Commission on Excellence in Education, *A Nation at Risk: The Imperative for Educational Reform* (Washington, D.C.: The Commission, 1983).

26. U.S. Department of Education, *Alliance for Excellence: Librarians Respond to 'A Nation at Risk'* (Washington, D.C.: U.S. Department of Education, 1984).

27. National Institute of Education, Study Group on Conditions of Excellence in American Higher Education, *Involvement in Learning: Realizing the Potential of American Higher Education* (Washington, D.C.: National Institute of Education, 1991).

28. Project on Redefining the Meaning and Purpose of Baccalaureate Degrees, *Integrity in the College Curriculum: A Report to the Academic Community* (Washington, D.C.: Association of American Colleges, 1985).

29. *America 2000: An Education Strategy: Sourcebook* (Washington, D.C.: U.S. Department of Education, 1991).

30. Ernest L. Boyer, *College: The Undergraduate Experience in America* (New York: Harper & Row, 1987), 160–61.

31. Larry L. Hardesty, *Faculty and the Library: The Undergraduate Experience* (Norwood, N.J.: Ablex, 1991).

32. Gresham Riley, "Myths and Realities: The Academic Viewpoint II," *College & Research Libraries* 45 (Sept. 1984): 367.

33. William A. Moffett, "Guest Editorial: Talking to Ourselves," *College & Research Libraries* 50 (Nov. 1989): 609–10.

34. For example, M. Kathy Cook, "Rank, Status, and Contributions of Academic Librarians As Perceived by the Teaching Faculty at Southern Illinois University, Carbondale," *College & Research Libraries* 42 (May 1981): 214–23; John Budd and Patricia Coutant, *Faculty Perceptions of Librarians: A Survey, 1980*, (ERIC, ED 215 697.

35. Gaby Divay, Ada M. Davis, and Nicole Michaud-Oystryk, "Faculty Perceptions of Librarians at the University of Manitoba," *College & Research Libraries* 48 (Jan. 1987): 27–35.

36. Bill Crowley, "Redefining the Status of the Librarian," *College & Research Libraries* 57 (Mar. 1996): 119.

37. Charles E. Slattery, "Faculty Status: Another 100 Years of Dialogue? Lessons from the Library School Closings," *Journal of Academic Librarianship* 20 (Sept. 1994): 193–94.

38. Bruce R. Kingma and Gillian M. McCombs, "The Opportunity Costs of Faculty Status for Academic Librarians," *College & Research Libraries* 56 (May 1995): 258, 263.

39. Frances Hopkins, "Bibliographic Instruction: An Emerging Professional Discipline," in *Directions for the Decade: Library Instruction in the 1980s*, ed. Carolyn A. Kirkendall (Ann Arbor, Mich.: Pierian, 1981), 13–24.

40. Michael Keresztesi, "The Science of Bibliography: Theoretical Implications for Bibliographic Instruction," in *Theories of Bibliographic Education: De-*

signs for Teaching, eds. Cerise Oberman and Katina Strauch (New York: Bowker, 1982), 1–26.

41. Trudi E. Jacobson and John R. Vallely, "A Half-Built Bridge: The Unfinished Work of Bibliographic Instruction," *Journal of Academic Librarianship* 17 (Jan. 1992): 362.

42. Parson, "User Perspective on a New Paradigm for Librarianship," 37.

43. Robert F. Munn, "The Bottomless Pit, or the Academic Library As Viewed from the Administration Building," *College & Research Libraries* 29 (Jan. 1968): 51–54, reprinted in *College & Research Libraries* 50 (Nov. 1989): 635–37; page references are to reprint edition, 51. Also Arthur M. McAnally and Robert B. Downs, "The Changing Role of Directors of University Libraries," *College & Research Libraries* 34 (Mar. 1973): 111.

44. Boyer, *College: The Undergraduate Experience in America,* 163.

45. Anne Woodsworth, "Getting Off the Library Merry-Go-Round: McAnally and Downs Revisited," *Library Journal* 114 (May 1989): 36.

46. Boyer, *College: The Undergraduate Experience in America,* 163.

47. Martin M. Cummings, *The Economics of Research Libraries* (Washington, D.C.: Council on Library Resources, 1986).

48. For a more detailed view of the budgetary changes over the past thirty years, see tables presented in Anthony M. Cummings et al., *University Libraries and Scholarly Communication: A Study Prepared for the Andrew W. Mellon Foundation* (Washington, D.C.: ARL, 1992).

49 Allen B. Veaner, "1985 to 1995: The Next Decade of Academic Librarianship, Part 1," *College & Research Libraries* 46 (May 1985): 213.

50. Kenneth E. Flower, ed. *Academic Libraries on the Periphery: How Telecommunications Information Policy Is Determined in Universities.* Occasional Paper No. 11 (Washington, D.C.: ARL, Office of Management Studies, 1986), 2.

51. John Perry and Anne Woodsworth, "Innovation and Change: Can We Learn from Corporate Models?" *Journal of Academic Librarianship* 21 (Mar. 1995): 117.

52. Nancy Allen and James F. Williams III, "Managing Technology: Innovation: Who's in Charge Here?" *Journal of Academic Librarianship* 20 (July 1994): 167.

53. Gary M. Pitkin, ed. *Information Management and Organizational Change in Higher Education* (Westport, Conn.: Meckler, 1992).

54. Susan K. Martin, "Information Technology and Libraries: Toward the Year 2000," *College & Research Libraries* 50 (July 1989): 404.

55. McAnally and Downs, "The Changing Role of Directors of University Libraries," 110.

56. Woodsworth, "Getting Off the Library Merry-Go-Round," 36.

57. Munn, "The Bottomless Pit," 635.

58. See, for example, Amusi Odi, "Creative Research and Theory Building in Library and Information Sciences," *College & Research Libraries* 43 (July 1982):

312–19; Helen A. Howard, "Organization Theory and Its Applications in Research in Librarianship," *Library Trends* 22 (spring 1984): 477–93.

59. Riley, "Myths and Realities"; Robert M. O'Neil, "Academic Libraries and the Future: A President's View," *College & Research Libraries* 47 (May 1984): 184–88.

60. Irene B. Hoadley, Sheila Creth, and Herbert S. White, "Reactions to 'Defining the Academic Librarian,'" *College & Research Libraries* 46 (Nov. 1985): 476.

61. Munn, "The Bottomless Pit," 637.

62. Larry L. Hardesty and David Kaser, "What Do Academic Administrators Think about the Library?" A Summary Report to the Council on Library Resources (Grant CLS 8018-A, Feb. 1990, photocopy), 2, 3, 4.

63. Quoted in Howard, "Organization Theory and Its Applications in Research in Librarianship," 477.

64. Jay M. Shafritz and J. Steven Ott, *Classics of Organization Theory*, 2nd. ed., rev. and expanded (Pacific Grove, Calif.: Brooks/Cole, 1987), 9.

65. Howard, "Organization Theory and Its Applications in Research in Librarianship," 489.

66. Odi, "Creative Research and Theory Building in Library and Information Sciences," 313. For further discussion of research in academic library management utilizing organization theory as a conceptual framework, see Deborah Jeanne Grimes, "Centrality and the Academic Library" (Ph.D. diss., University of Alabama, 1993).

67. Howard, "Organization Theory and Its Applications in Research Librarianship," 487.

68. Gerald R. Salancik and Jeffrey Pfeffer, "The Bases and Uses of Power in Organizational Decision-Making: The Case of the University," *Administrative Science Quarterly* 19 (Dec. 1974): 453–73.

69. Hanna Ashar, "Internal and External Variables and Their Effect on a University's Retrenchment Decisions: Two Theoretical Perspectives" (Ph.D. diss., University of Washington, 1987).

70. Hanna Ashar and Jonathan Z. Shapiro, "Measuring Centrality: A Note on Hackman's Resource Allocation Theory," *Administrative Science Quarterly* 33 (June 1988): 281.

71. Cummings, *The EconomicSs of Research Libraries*.

72. Cummings et al., *University Libraries and Scholarly Communication*.

2. Centrality in Organization Theory

I f, as proposed in chapter 1, academic library centrality is the key to understanding and achieving the academic library mission, it is a concept that librarians cannot afford to overlook or misunderstand. An understanding of centrality is important not only for practice but also for generating theory in librarianship. In managing and planning for libraries, theory is useful "not to mirror reality but to help explain it." Good theory, in turn, leads to good practice because it predicts the outcomes of actions and it helps explain relationships.[1] Although librarianship has very little theory of its own, academic librarians are fortunate that organization theory can help them understand centrality and its related concepts more clearly. Organization theory provides insight into the concept of centrality, as other academic units have defined it. This definition goes beyond the notion of centrality as mission congruence. Organization theory also gives a clearer perspective of the larger organization in which the academic library exists. This chapter begins by tracking key concepts related to centrality through the history of organization theory. Then, focusing on higher education, it examines the important concepts drawn from studies of retrenchment and resource allocation. This discussion moves to studies of departmental or subunit power and, ultimately, to definitions of centrality. Following this route leads through the existing theory toward a better understanding of academic library centrality. In the end, the author hopes to lay a foundation for improvements in academic library practice.

A Brief Overview of Organization Theory

One time line of organization theory goes back to the Old Testament account of Jethro instructing Moses on the delegation of authority over the tribes of Israel. Sun Tzu's *The Art of War* is an early treatise on hierarchical organization, whereas Machiavelli's *The Prince* is the first how-to-succeed book for managers.[2] Most organization theorists, however, begin the discussion of organization theory with a chronological grouping of schools: classical (through the 1930s); neoclassical (1940s through 1950s); and contemporary (1960s to the present).

Although the contemporary schools contribute directly to an understanding of library centrality, the neoclassical school also provides important concepts. Spawned in the 1700s by the British Factory system and the Industrial Revolution, the classical school of organization theory was dominant in both literature and practice through the 1930s. Linked with the harsh societal values of its origins, the classical school emphasizes formal organization and is characterized as rigid and mechanistic. Classicists proposed that organizations function "one best way."[3] By the 1930s, however, neoclassicists found that organizations were much more complex and the "machine model" of the classicists lost its appeal. Changing societal values reflected a more concerned and compassionate view of the ways in which people work together, and human relations became an important element in neoclassical organizational practice and theory. In addition to this emphasis on human relations, the neoclassicists stressed the dynamic, or changing, quality of organizations and their interactions with their environments.

One of the most challenging and influential of the neoclassical theorists was Herbert A. Simon. His publication in 1946 of "The Proverbs of Administration" focused on decision-making and outlined a theory of "bounded rationality."[4] Bounded rationality implies that there are limits to what the decision maker can know about any given situation. In other words, the decision maker cannot seek the optimum solution but attempts instead to work within realistic boundaries or constraints. Internal constraints include the decision maker's intellectual capabilities, training, experience, and motivation. External constraints include influence from others within the organization as well as outside the organization. Neoclassicists R. M. Cyert and James G. March not only focused on decision-making in the study of organizations but also identified the important organizational behaviors of coalition-building and negotiation. *Coalition-building* refers to the sometimes temporary alliances developed by organizational units, such as departments, in order to gain more power within the organization; *negotiation* is the process used by coalitions to bargain and trade in order to achieve their individual goals. Coalition-building and negotiation are dynamic organizational behaviors that change as individual unit goals change.[5] The first view of organizations as "equilibrium systems," that is, systems functioning within and defined by changing environments, came from Talcott Parsons.[6] Parsons further observed that all organizations must adapt to their environments, must achieve goals, must integrate various subunits, and must maintain values over time. Parsons related organizational values (i.e., goals) to decision-making and the ways in which organizations operate. He viewed the allocation of resources within the organization as a means of "value implementation." Three concepts important to an understanding of academic library centrality are drawn from these neoclassical organization theorists: the vitality or dynamic quality of organizations; the influence of environment on the organization; and decision-making, with its limitations of bounded rationality, as an indication of organization values. Figure 1, which illustrates these contributions from neoclassical organization theory, is the first in a series of models in this chapter that show how these concepts are related to academic library centrality.

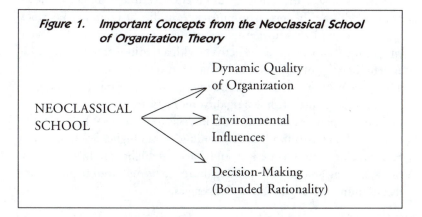

Figure 1. Important Concepts from the Neoclassical School of Organization Theory

NEOCLASSICAL SCHOOL

Dynamic Quality of Organization

Environmental Influences

Decision-Making (Bounded Rationality)

The three most relevant contemporary schools of organization theory are the systems school, the contingency school, and the power/politics school. The roots of the systems school of organization theory lie in the studies of Ludwig von Bertanlanffy on general systems theory and on the model of Norbert Weiner, with its important concept of feedback or self-regulation.[7] In the 1960s, systems theory dominated the study of organizations. Intuitively simple, systems theory defines organizations in terms of interconnecting components, including inputs, outputs, processes, feedback loops, and environment.[8] In open systems, environment is extremely important, allowing factors external to the organization to influence its components, particularly inputs and processes. A key concept in systems theory is "equifinality," which means there are numerous ways to achieve a particular end. Equifinality replaces the classicists' rigid concept of "one best way," emphasizing instead the value of different organizational structures for different types of organizations.[9] Systems theory is the underlying assumption of almost all current organizational study today, reaching every important movement since 1960.[10]

Called a "close cousin" of the systems school of organization theory, the contingency school emphasizes the effects of shifting environments or external factors on the organization.[11] For example, A. H. Walker and Jay W. Lorsch offered evidence that an organization's environment determines whether its product or its function is the better basis for the organization's structure.[12] Dubbing this perspective "contingency theory," Paul R. Lawrence and Jay Lorsch proposed that different organizational structures or processes are *contingent* upon conditions or environments; that is, an organization may be more effective under different conditions or within different environments.[13] Studies at London's Tavistock Institute in the 1960s further indicated that organizations within stable environments operate most effectively with a traditional mechanistic hierarchy having formal rules and structured decision-making. Unstable environments, on the other hand, require a more organic form of organizational structure, with less rigidity, more reliance on employees, and more participation from employees in decision-making.[14] Jay Galbraith discovered that organizations functioning within higher levels of uncertainty (i.e., environmental instability) require higher levels of information; planning and decision-making under such conditions require a flexible examination of possible contingencies.[15]

Although evident within the contingency school of organization theory, the interrelatedness of units within the organization (as in the systems view) and the formation of coalitions between units that negotiate during decision-making are the cornerstones of the power/politics school of organization theory. By the end of the 1960s, the power/politics views dominated both bureaucratic and human relations schools of theory.[16] Drawing on the neoclassical studies of Cyert and March, the power/politics school rejects the assumptions that organizations are driven by general goals or formal authority.[17] Instead, the power/politics organization consists of complex systems of coalitions, which are in continuous conflict over influence and resources within the organization. In fact, from the power/politics viewpoint, organizational goals shift according to the "balance of power among coalitions."[18]

Despite a lack of consensus, there is a considerable body of literature on the role of power and politics within organizations. James D. Thompson, for example, observed that the lack of balance between units within the organization creates the need for power play.[19] In 1985, John P. Kotter argued that formal authority is not the only source of organizational power and that power points in all directions—not just down the hierarchy.[20] He and others related power to dependence, suggesting that organizations will suffer prima donnas because lower level employees can wield influence through expertise, charisma, coalition-building, and effort. Figure 2 shows that important concepts of the neoclassical school—the dynamic quality of organizations, environmental influences, and the importance of decision-making—carry forward through the systems school, the contingency school, and the power/politics school. These, in turn, point toward subunit or departmental power within the organization. The significant concepts are the open systems view (of interacting units, including environmental influences), equifinality (i.e., more than one means of achieving a goal), the effects of different environments, and contingencies on an organization's effectiveness, interrelatedness of organizational units, and coalitional negotiation between units and its effects on decision-making. All these concepts, illustrated in figure 2, are qualities associated with the organization as a whole rather than as an individual unit or department within the organization.

For example, we can characterize political organizations as open systems whose components are influenced by external contingencies and

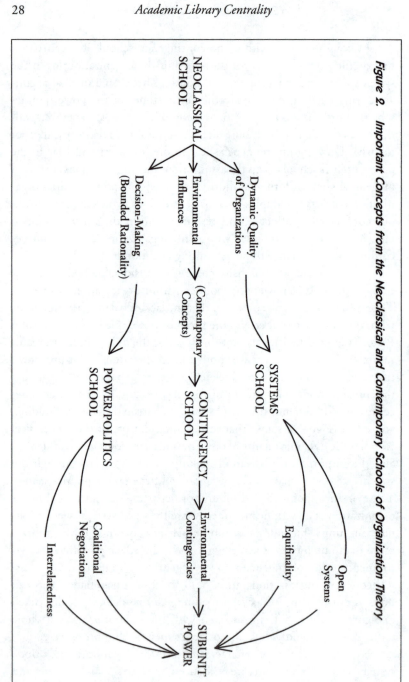

Figure 2. Important Concepts from the Neoclassical and Contemporary Schools of Organization Theory

the environment. Political organizations consist of interrelated units or departments that develop mutually beneficial coalitions. These coalitions negotiate in decision-making to achieve greater influence or to acquire more institutional resources. The overriding quality of a political organization is that it is a living organism, not an inflexible machine, and that change will have an impact on the organization's structure, coalitions, and decision-making. How these organizational qualities relate to the degree of power held by a department or subunit, such as the academic library, and then to centrality, is described below.

Universities as Organizations

Before proceeding in the search for better understanding of academic library centrality, it is important to consider the special characteristics of universities as complex organizations. Internally, both the academic library and the university function through professional, dual hierarchies. In the university, the administrative hierarchy, through which the business of the university is conducted and through which financial decisions are made, leads up through the office of the president and then to the board of trustees. The educational hierarchy, which leads up through more egalitarian departments and faculty senates, generally has authority over course and program content.[21] The dual hierarchy in the academic library operates similarly. The library's administrative hierarchy deals with financial and management procedures and policy implementation; its professional hierarchy deals with professional issues and responsibilities (i.e., selection, services, user assistance, cataloging, bibliography, and instruction).

In addition, the academic library and the university function within several larger organizations or systems simultaneously. For instance, a university is often part of a larger system at the state level, and it may participate in large consortia that include several academic institutions. The academic library also functions within larger organizations or systems. For example, it is part of formal bibliographic systems and consortia and, like its parent university, is part of the larger system of scholarly communication. As W. Boyd Rayward pointed out, "the library is always part of another organization that provides it with its raison d'être and with financial support."[22]

Although academic organizations are open systems, they have distinguishing characteristics. J. Victor Baldridge et al. demonstrated that academic organizations such as universities have "vague, ambiguous goals" which require their administrators to "grapple with a higher degree of uncertainty and conflict."[23] University goals (i.e., library goals) are not concerned with maximizing profit; instead, they deal with the more intangible "products" of teaching, research, and service. As a result, organizational relationships within universities cannot be studied in exactly the same manner as organizational relationships in business and industry.[24]

By definition, universities are collections of departments, colleges, and schools. The basic unit of academic organization is the academic department representing a specific field or discipline. Because academic units necessarily have their own goals and priorities, some theorists characterize academic organizations as "organized anarchies," defining them as "system[s] with little central coordination or control."[25]

Frederick S. Hills and Thomas A. Mahoney proposed that academic organizations, despite a unifying organizational mission, are "loosely coupled groups" that may have conflicting goals and may also compete for resources to accomplish these goals.[26]

As organized anarchies, universities also fit the political model of organization, in which power and influence shift between coalitions and interest groups, whose compositions change over time. The decision process in political organizations is disorderly, depending upon the push and pull of interests. The overriding ideology is struggle and conflict, with some departments rising as winners and others falling as losers. In other words, "conflict is legitimate and expected."[27] The realities of university governance sometimes contradict the "myth of consensus" shared by many members of the university community, as stated by Dwight R. Ladd:

> . . . for better or for worse the university is made up of and functions for a congeries of interest groups that do not share a basic consensus about the institution's values, goals, processes, and who are quite regularly in conflict.[28]

In addition to conflict among departments, others—students, faculty, and outside groups (such as boards of trustees)—make demands on the university unlike those made on nonacademic organizations.[29] To a certain extent, other demands arise from professionalism, which affects the value system of faculty and their views of university priorities. This is equally true for librarians who function within the academic library and within the university; it is a situation further complicated by the strong service values librarians hold.[30] Because of these competing interests and values within universities and their libraries, we can use a power/politics definition of organization with recognition of the special characteristics of the academic organization identified in the preceding discussion. The university, then, fits the organization characterized in figure 2. In addition, the special characteristics of the academic organization just identified relate to resource allocation, retrenchment, power, and centrality, which are described in detail below.

Resource Allocation, Retrenchment, and Power

The literature reviewed above not only describes research on decision-making in organizations and the special characteristics of universities as organizations, it also points out important organizational qualities that enable subunits or departments to exercise power and influence within the organization. We must look to studies in resource allocation and retrenchment for further insight into the ways in which universities define central or core units and especially to the qualities of subunits themselves that contribute to the degree of power they hold within the larger organization. Detailed examination of the role played by subunit or departmental power in university decision-making will provide additional insight into the concept of centrality.

Resource Allocation

Decision-making in the area of resource allocation is an important, relatively young area of study within the power/politics school of organization theory, particularly in the study of universities as organizations. In most studies of organizations, resource allocation is distinguished from the process of budgeting. Budgeting is the fiscal accounting of incomes and expenditures, usually limited by time (annually, quarterly, monthly).[31] Most organizational budgeting during periods of abundance is incremental; that is, it depends on history and precedence.[32] In general, budgeting follows the mechanistic models of classical organization theory, which assumes an omniscient decision maker who optimizes resource distribution within the organization.[33]

By the 1970s, the budgetary flexibility that went hand in hand with the financial abundance of the preceding decade was lost. The only flexibility remaining in institutions of higher education lay in internal reallocation, or resource allocation, of available funds.[34] Reallocation was the method by which the institution coped with the gap between revenue and expenditures,[35] and the share of institutional resources—including space, location, personnel, and funds—allocated to a unit.[36] Raymond F. Zammuto suggested that periods of scarcity bring hidden conflicts into the open, making resource allocation a struggle in which gains by one unit result in losses for another.[37]

Unlike studies of budgeting, recent studies of resource allocation adopt three primary concepts: the neoclassical concept of bounded rationality; the contemporary concept of open systems, which suggests that goals are difficult to determine and consequently that competing goals limit options;[38] and the contemporary model of the political, coalitional organization.[39] Baltes, for example, characterized the initial stage of resource allocation as political, noting that it becomes more rational over time.[40] Others observe that, as political decisions, short-term budget cuts are merely "dysfunctional" attempts to preserve a status quo; ultimately, such cuts threaten the quality of all academic programs.[41]

One means through which universities rationalized resource allocation decisions was program review, a comparison of departmental contributions to the university's goals and mission. In many cases, the term *centrality* was used. A study by James Hyatt et al. for the National Association of College and University Business Officers (NACUBO) reviewed the reallocation process in five colleges and universities in three states hit hardest by revenue shortfalls in the early 1980s.[42] Schools that expected inadequate revenues for a long time made larger budget cuts in administrative and peripheral units than in units determined to be central to the institution. The determination of which units were central was based, in part, on program review or "need," which Hyatt et al. defined as centrality. Similarly, Mortimer and Tierney found that "centrality to mission" frequently appears in university program review criteria.[43] Although centrality to the institutional mission was used imprecisely and often ambiguously in these contexts, it emerged as one criterion by which universities evaluated programs during a resource allocation process.[44]

University Retrenchment

By the late 1970s and early 1980s, program review took on even more significance. Studies showed that when the duration of the fiscal crisis lengthened, universities moved along a continuum from simple resource allocation toward the development of more complex retrenchment policies. These policies grew from substantive program review and change.[45] In general, *retrenchment* means the discontinuance of programs or a process for targeting programs for reduction or elimination.[46] Retrenchment may involve program mergers, elimination of degrees or programs within departments, and/or the discontinuance of entire departments.[47] Studies show that institutions involved in retrenchment programs have developed specific criteria to guide decision-making. In some cases, criteria relate to program review; in others, they are proactive strategies to reduce the threat of retrenchment in specific academic units.

Of particular interest to academic librarians are analyses of retrenchment in graduate schools of library and information science. Between 1978 and 1993, fourteen schools were closed or consolidated into other academic units. Although the impact of these closings on the profession of librarianship is significant, library school closings also have implications for the academic library.[48] Marianne Cooper and Shoshana Kaufman suggested, for example, that the academic community has a difficult time distinguishing between the library school and the campus library.[49] Confusion over the roles of the library school and the campus library suggests that similar criteria may apply in program review for both. In institutions where the library school does not withstand retrenchment program review, the reputation or standing of the campus library also may be in jeopardy.

Marion Paris and Karen Feingold Ceppos showed that financial exigency alone was not the sole reason for library school closings.[50] They found, instead, that there were several motivations for university decisions to close the library school: isolation of the library school within the university; unresponsive or complacent leadership within the library school; conflicts with stronger academic units over program content or students; lack of program innovation; and poor program reviews according to university-wide criteria. Deans and directors of fifty-eight schools of library and information studies in the United States and Canada cited similar criteria, including centrality to the university mission and/or priorities, to be significant criteria against which programs are reviewed.[51] The experiences of library schools are representative of general trends in retrenchment programs in all areas of study.

Criteria used in the review of academic programs, including library schools, fall into three major categories: quality, cost-effectiveness, and need. *Quality* generally refers to the quality of faculty and staff, students (both enrollees and graduates), facilities and equipment, and support services (such as administrative support or library resources). Quality is reflected in regional and national reputation, the level or position achieved by graduates, productivity by faculty in both teaching and research, and the acquisition of outside funding (often linked with reputation).[52] *Cost-effectiveness* refers to cost–revenue relationships, tuition income, effectiveness of program management, use of program resources, cost per graduate, and program productivity. Cost-effectiveness relates also to acquisition of outside funding.[53] These criteria are often cited as measures of program quality as well. *Need* is the third major aspect of academic program review, and because it relates to centrality, it is the most relevant to the study of the academic library. Need is demonstrated through several factors, including student demand, geographical uniqueness or demand, employment demand for graduates, and centrality.[54]

Although the criteria for program review overlap, centrality is frequently cited in both resource allocation and retrenchment decisions. A review of resource allocation and retrenchment in higher education gives an idea of the values held by the university and how it uses those values to distribute resources when finances are limited. Centrality is one of those values, and it is related to power, especially to *subunit* power, within the organization. Figure 3 shows the relationships between centrality and its components drawn from the review of resource allocation and retrenchment studies. The following discussion of subunit power illus-

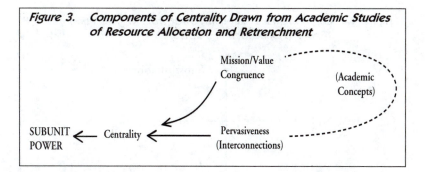

Figure 3.   Components of Centrality Drawn from Academic Studies of Resource Allocation and Retrenchment

trates how an academic department preserves its power during times of resource scarcity.

Subunit or Departmental Power

Although *power* is a difficult term to define, most of us have no problem recognizing power and can readily identify which individuals or groups have it. Power relies on relationships or context and on the elements of conflict or competition.[55] In the present discussion, power is viewed as a predictor of "changes and shifts in decisions and allocations."[56] The following observation seems particularly appropriate to this discussion of subunit power within the university:

> Power . . . is defined as the ability to influence organizational
> decisions . . . . Therefore, the power of an academic department
> is the department's ability to influence college decisions so that
> the decisions reflect departmental interests and preferences.[57]

The study of subunit power within organizations began with Michel Crozier's observation that the subunit that reduces uncertainty is the most influential within the organization.[58] Perrow was the first to shift research from individual to subunit or departmental power within an organization.[59] He found that although critical functions vary by organization, the unit that performs "the most critical function tends to have the most power." Building on these findings and others, Hickson and his colleagues developed the seminal theory for subunit power, proposing a strategic contingencies theory of power.[60] From this perspective, subunit power results from the interaction of three contingencies

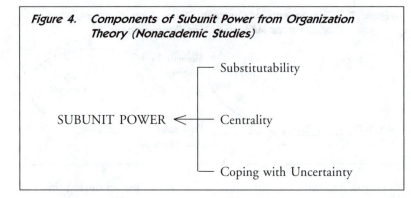

Figure 4.   Components of Subunit Power from Organization Theory (Nonacademic Studies)

(or dependencies between units): coping with uncertainty, low substitutability, and centrality. These components are illustrated in figure 4 .

Uncertainty is "lack of information about future events, so that alternatives and their outcomes are unpredictable."[61] Coping with uncertainty may occur through prevention or routinization, which tends to lessen both uncertainty and power, or through effective action, which reduces the *impact* of uncertainty but increases power (e.g., those who fight fires are more influential than those who prevent them). Although organizations do not seek to eliminate uncertainty, they do seek to control it. For example, in the French tobacco factories studied by Crozier, maintenance engineers provided routine maintenance on factory equipment to ensure that it would perform predictably.[62] In this way, the maintenance engineers reduced the uncertainty of production for the factory and made the related activities of other organizational units predictable. The maintenance engineers coped with uncertainty through routine maintenance as well as through effective action taken to repair equipment when it malfunctioned. *Substitutability*, on the other hand, refers to the alternatives that subunits may have for acquiring the resources of another subunit. In the French tobacco factories, no substitutes for the maintenance engineers were available; therefore, their substitutability within the organization was low and they were an extremely important organizational unit. The third contingency, *centrality*, is not used by Hickson et al. to mean mission congruence as in retrenchment and reallocation studies.[63] Instead, centrality is a combination of work flow pervasiveness (i.e., connections between units or the degree to which one unit interacts with another) and immediacy or criticality of a subunit's resources for other subunits (i.e., the speed with which the actions or outputs of one unit affect another unit's actions or the degree to which the actions or outputs of one unit affect others). Although the maintenance engineers in the tobacco factories had little direct interaction with other departments (i.e., low pervasiveness), their work had immediate and critical effects on almost every department (i.e., high immediacy and criticality). In other words, if the maintenance engineers did not do their jobs, no one else could do his or her job. Control of these three contingencies, then, determines the degree of influence a subunit holds within the organization. These components are illustrated in figure 5.

C. R. Hinings, et al. confirmed strategic contingencies theory in a study of breweries and container companies.[64] Their findings further suggested that subunit power is linked first with coping with uncertainty (as the single best predictor of subunit power), then with immediacy (one component of centrality), then with substitutability, and finally with pervasiveness (a second component of centrality). Keith G. Provan also argued persuasively that departmental power is a strategic contingency on which institutional decision-making hinges.[65] Noting that the earlier study did not address a means of measuring centrality, which was one of the key concepts, Carol S. Saunders and Richard Scamell replicated the work of Hinings et al. in a study of six universities and four oil and gas companies.[66] Although their findings were consistent with the original study by Hickson and his colleagues, Saunders and Scamell noted that there appears to be a difference between the relative importance associated with each strategic contingency when applied to universities, where the work flow is informational. In this situation, where critical information is obtained through

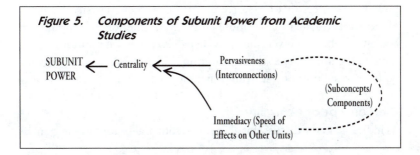

Figure 5. Components of Subunit Power from Academic Studies

intraorganizational contacts, they found immediacy (or criticalilty) to be less important than pervasiveness (or interconnectedness). In other words, critical information in universities is exchanged through internal contacts. In this environment, the immediacy or criticality of a department's resources is less important than its connections within the university to other departments.

Strategic contingencies theory has been applied in other non-production-oriented organizations such as health care organizations. For example, Bruce J. Fried studied intraorganizational *group* power (not departmental or unit power) in twenty ambulatory care units and found that physicians and nurses gained power by exerting influence over different contingencies (physicians through nonsubstitutability and nurses through centrality and coping with organizational uncertainties).[67] In a study of nine Israeli health care clinics with three subunits each, Iris Cohen and Ran Lachman found the same relationship between subunit power and its subconcepts. They found that coping with uncertainty and pervasiveness were key predictors of subunit influence.[68] In a longitudinal study of the same health care clinics, however, Lachman concluded that a previous power position, or history, within the organization was the chief predictor of subunit power over time, rather than control of contingencies.[69]

A number of studies of subunit power in higher education adopted a strategic contingencies viewpoint, especially in relation to university resource allocation. Hills and Mahoney conducted the first of these studies, identifying power criteria (rather than universalistic criteria) as the independent variable influencing resource allocation in times of financial austerity.[70] Pfeffer and Salancik applied strategic contingencies theory to the study of university resource allocation and determined that academic unit or departmental power reflects the extent to which the unit provides resources that are scarce or critical to the university.[71] Finally, Hackman and Ashar placed more emphasis on the role of centrality in academic subunit power and provided theory-based definitions applicable to the university as an organization.[72] Figure 5 illustrates the components of subunit power from nonacademic studies.

The Concept of Centrality

As indicated in the discussions above on resource allocation and retrenchment, centrality is one important means used by university administrators to determine priorities for resource allocation in times of prolonged financial austerity. Given the economic outlook for the American university for the future, it is important to understand centrality as used in organization theory in relation to both the academic department and the academic library. Furthermore, as an underlying assumption stated in the 1989 "Standards for University Libraries: Evaluation of Performance" of the Association of College and Research Libraries,[73] centrality is also a pivotal point on which the mission of the academic library turns. Assessing the success of any academic library, then, requires some means of assessing academic library centrality. The systematic analysis of centrality in organization theory that follows will lead to a clearer understanding of academic library centrality.

As indicated in the preceding discussion of strategic contingencies theory and subunit power, Hickson et al. identified centrality as one of three strategic contingencies that affect subunit influence within an organization.[74] Centrality interacts with the other two strategic contingencies, which are the extent to which the organizational unit is able to cope with uncertainty and the extent of the substitutability of its actions or resources within the organization. To hold power, any subunit must have a minimum of centrality; increased centrality contributes to greater subunit power. In simplest terms, Saunders and Scamell defined *organizational centrality* as "the flow of information and work between departments."[75] Lachman offered more detail:

> The division of organizational work among subunits creates an interactive and interdependent system in which some units are more central than others. Subunits connected with many other units are considered to have more control over flows in tasks, social interaction, or communication networks and, therefore, are potentially more powerful.[76]

Hickson et al. suggested that centrality actually consists of two components, or subconcepts: "workflow pervasiveness" and "immediacy."[77] The first of these components, *pervasiveness*, refers to the "degree to which the workflows of a subunit connect with the workflows of other subunits . . ." or "the extent of task interactions."

As an open system, an organization consists of numerous interactive subunits; the extent of interactivity between subunits determines the extent of pervasiveness. Sid Huff applied the term *interconnectedness*, stating that:

> [t]he more one department has to interact with all the others, the more central it is to the organization. Greater centrality implies greater overall dependence of the organization on that unit.[78]

In terms of contemporary business organizations, for example, the systems or data-processing office of a manufacturing firm generally manages all organizational information. Its activities are connected to virtually every department that utilizes the firm's computer system (e.g., inventory control, production, public relations, accounting, payroll, personnel, quality control, distribution, transportation, and management). As a result, the systems office is highly pervasive to the organization. The same may be said for a university computing center through which all computer and telecommunications technologies are centralized for the institution.

The second component of centrality is *immediacy*, which was defined by Hickson et al. as "the speed and severity with which the workflows of a subunit affect the final outputs of the organization." In other words, centrality depends upon how essential the subunit's activities are "in the sense that their cessation would quickly and substantially impede the primary workflow of the organization."[79] Speed need not be measured in hours or even days; Hinings et al. found that the speed with which the work of one organizational unit affects another may be measured along a continuum of weeks.[80] Speed, or immediacy, is easily demonstrated. In Crozier's study, for instance, the activities of the maintenance engineers in the French tobacco factories—or lack of them—had an immediate and severe impact on the organization's final output: If the maintenance engineers did not keep the equipment running, there was no production. With no production, there was no work for others within the organization.[81] Using the contemporary illustration of the systems office again, a manufacturing firm in today's information-rich environment is dependent upon the expertise of its systems personnel to keep the organization productive. Consequently, the systems office in a manufacturing firm exemplifies subunit centrality: Not only are its activities pervasive to the entire organization, its activities have an immediate effect on the ultimate output of the organization. It is considered a central or core organizational subunit; as such, it garners a great deal of organizational power.[82] So far, centrality and its components, pervasiveness and immediacy, have been reviewed within the general organization. The following section takes a closer look at centrality in academic units within the university organization.

Academic Unit Centrality within the University

Both Hickson et al. and Saunders and Scamell suggested that work flows, and therefore centrality, differ in information-based organizations such as universities. Several other authors have emphasized organizational mission or value congruence in defining centrality in the university.[83] Definitions of centrality with these emphases often vaguely reference the university's formal mission statement, administrative values, and core or mainstream programs or activities. For example, the criteria established by the University of Michigan for reallocation decisions included the following: "[p]rogram's centrality to institution's mission, viewed in terms of its pertinence to and support of growth, preservation, and communication of knowledge." Similarly, the University of Idaho cited "centrality to institution's mission" as a criterion for program elimination or reduction.[84] Kathleen M. Heim and J. Keith Ostertag defined *centrality* as the "measure of a unit's importance to the fundamental mission of the organization," noting that no university can exist without English, mathematics, or chemistry departments.[85]

Gaughan found centrality to be "a term commonly used . . . but seldom defined," albeit the basis of program review in many institutions.[86] Without explicitly using the term *centrality*, Herbert S. White observed that the "value system" of the university must be shared by the academic unit in order for it to survive retrenchment.[87] Similarly, Margaret F. Stieg suggested that congruence with the university administration's values is important in avoiding retrenchment: "Faculty and schools must prove that what they are doing is worthwhile in terms of management values."[88] Suggesting that program review *begins* with mission review, Zammuto stated that:

[c]oncensus is important because the mission statement is one of the yardsticks against which the centrality of individual programs to an institution is measured during the program review process.[89]

This review process, he said, "enables an institution to assess the fit between academic programs and the institution's mission . . . ."[90] In a similar vein, Kent John Chabotar and James P. Honan suggested that university mission statements are beginning to reflect "a more selective 'boutique' model" that focuses resources on those programs viewed as "more central to the organization's mission."[91] Concentrating on what the institution *should* be doing, Lincoln and Tuttle indicated that centrality, defined in terms of the institution's "core mission," is a criterion that should be applied prior to assessing all programs. They stated that "[w]hen institutional survival is threatened, no program that is not central to that mission ought to be retained."[92]

More specifically, Hackman defined *centrality* as "how closely a unit's purpose matches those central to the organization."[93] As her "pivotal concept," this definition assumed that the university is an open, political system of coalitions competing for scarce resources. Hackman identified, along an unspecified continuum, core units as those whose functions are essential to the definition of the organization. Without the core, the organization will have another overall purpose.

Peripheral units were defined as those "noncentral parts of the institution," which vary widely in size and individual mission. Hackman argued that if the mission of the university is to educate and to conduct research, all academic units meet the definition of "core" unit. She reported that core units gained resources when their budget negotiation strategies emphasized their own needs (because the unit is already of central importance to the university's mission). Peripheral units, she discovered, gained resources when their negotiation strategies emphasized broader, institutional needs and especially when they gained outside resources required by the university during periods of scarcity.[94]

A few practitioner reports on peripheral units within the university suggested ways of changing the status of a department from peripheral to core. For example, J. Richard Polidoro presented a study of the Department of Physical Education, Health, and Recreation at the Univer-

sity of Rhode Island in which he set forth actions to reduce any academic department's risk of retrenchment.[95] Without defining the concept, he suggested that academic departments assert their centrality to
the university mission in a presentation to the university administration.
More directly on the issue of peripherality was the research of Stanley O.
Ikenberry and Renee C. Friedman on university institutes and centers.[96]
In a study of institutes and centers in every state in the United States,
they considered the nature and extent of interdisciplinary involvement
(between the institute/center and academic departments) and the domi-
nance of academic departments over institutes and centers. They identified differences in goals, organizational structures, procedures, and administrative roles of directors. As in the studies mentioned above, their
goal was to assist the practitioner in moving the institute or center from
the periphery to the core of the university.

Other university practitioners and researchers, however, associated
centrality more closely with the definitions regarding work flow rather
than mission.[97] For instance, another program review criterion used by
the University of Minnesota was "connectedness," which was defined as
follows:

> This somewhat awkward word refers to the extent to which the
> programs of a department or college serve other departments
> or colleges. Where this connectedness is high, it is unrealistic to
> consider extensive reductions in its activities unless alternative
> arrangements can be made to provide for the instructional or
> support activities.[98]

"Connectedness" has also been described in terms of an academic
department's service to other units within the university. For example,
California State University at Hayward measured connections between
departments as the percentage of classes taken by students outside their
major departments and used this measure in an evaluation of overstaff-
ing.[99] White suggested that connectedness involves participation in university-wide committees, interdisciplinary research, joint appointments,
and dual-degree programs.[100] In line with this, one of the reasons cited
by Columbia University for closing the oldest library school in the United
States was "isolation from the intellectual life of the community."[101] Ashar

viewed centrality as an independent variable that influences university resource allocation decisions.[102] Unlike Hackman, Ashar operationalized centrality in terms of work flows (referring to the definitions of Hickson et al., Hinings et al. and others). She defined *centrality* as "the quantity and intensity of a department's relations with other departments on campus." Ashar's definitions were reminiscent of the program review criteria adopted by the University of Minnesota, of research-based determinants of subunit power within the university, and of practitioner observations on service to other organizational units. She observed:

> In a university setting the workflows are research and teaching. A more central department will offer more classes that can be taken by students outside the department, its faculty will conduct more collaborative research with faculty of other departments, teach more collaborative classes, and so forth.

To measure centrality according to this definition, Ashar constructed a "centrality index" from the following components:
  1. ratio of nonmajor students to department majors;
  2. ratio of nonmajor students enrolled in a department's broad classes;
  3. number of research collaborations with other departments;
  4. number of teaching collaborations with other departments.
She assumed that the university has a broad institutional goal of providing a liberal education, requiring broad classes. Ashar's research showed that the ratio of nonmajor students to major students and the number of teaching collaborations are positively related to resource allocations. It also showed, unexpectedly, that a high ratio of nonmajor students enrolled in broad classes and a high number of research collaborations are negatively related to resource allocations. Despite the negative correlations, she found centrality, as manifested in connectedness between departments, to be second in importance to faculty productivity in explaining resource allocation decisions. She suggested that this is true because central units can rely on their connections and coalitions to provide a stable power base and because the organization tends to rely on intraorganizational connections more heavily during periods of financial distress. Thus, two major views of centrality within the university emerge: one focusing

on congruence with the university's mission; one focusing on interconnectedness and work flow connections.

Problems in Existing Definitions of Centrality

Despite the cogent research of Hackman and Ashar and related practitioner views, definitions of university department centrality and peripherality remain problematic in some areas. For example, academic departments can form strategic coalitions merely to gain or retain resources and to artificially increase their subunit influence. Connectivity can be quickly attained by one department by requiring students to take classes in another department. As a result, centrality can be manipulated by a department, regardless of the quality of the program or the actual need for the program.[103]

Subjectivity in defining centrality is also a problem. For example, Hackman's definition offers no objective means of distinguishing between core and peripheral units.[104] Melchiori asked: "Within the galaxy of offerings, how does one determine the degree of importance of any one discipline? Should it be placed by an ideal perception, and whose?"[105]

Lloyd G. Cooper echoed this concern in describing the retrenchment process, stating that the difficulty in retaining the "mainstream" activities of a university during a retrenchment process lies in "determining what is essential and what is not."[106] In addition, the interpretation of the university's mission is subjective. For example, Paris noted that a university may make changes in its mission to exclude certain programs.[107] A library school dean defined centrality as ". . . [t]he sum total of the agendas of the decision-makers in the university. Sometimes the mission is articulated by the president, such as 'high technology' or 'sponsored research.'"[108]

This definition implies a difference between the university's stated mission and its immediate priorities. According to Jeffrey Katzer, the central academic unit ". . . is seen by university administrators as being linked to the center of the current institution and poised to remain at the center of *where the university is heading in the future* [emphasis added]."[109]

Finally, these problems in defining centrality within the university compound to make measurement difficult. Hinings et al. did not develop a means of measuring centrality; Lachman did not measure immediacy, which is one of the two components of centrality; Hackman arbitrarily designated all academic units as core or central units within the university; and Ashar had difficulty in distinguishing between technical and substantive centrality in her work flow definition of centrality. Consequently, centrality remains a much-used, but inadequately measured, concept. As such, it is insufficiently, and perhaps inappropriately, used in departmental strategies for fighting negative resource allocation decisions. But despite problems in measuring centrality, it has proven a powerful concept for research in academic organizations and for universities conducting programmatic review. Figure 6 pulls together all the concepts traced through the history of organization theory that lead to subunit power and centrality.

Summary

The theoretical genealogy, outlined in figure 6, of the organizational concept "centrality" begins in the neoclassical school of organization theory, which contributes three important ideas: the dynamic quality of organizations, environmental influences, and decision-making based on bounded rationality. Breaking with the traditional views of organizations, neoclassicists found that successful organizations do not have "one best way" of performing tasks or achieving goals; instead, organizations are dynamic and changing. This change is the result of environmental influences, which can affect organizational processes, priorities, and structure. Neoclassicists also rejected the omniscient decision maker in favor of bounded rationality, in which the decision maker is not viewed as capable of determining the ultimate, all-inclusive decision, especially in consideration of environmental influences. Thus, decision-making, within bounded rationality and environmental influences, became a key issue in the study of organizations and how they operate.

The contemporary schools that drew from these concepts are the systems, contingency, and power/politics schools of organization theory. The systems school contributes the related concepts of open systems and equifinality. Open systems refer to the changing nature of the organization as a system or collection of interacting resources and processes. The university is an open system affected by the resources and processes that comprise it. Furthermore, equifinality, or the fact that there are

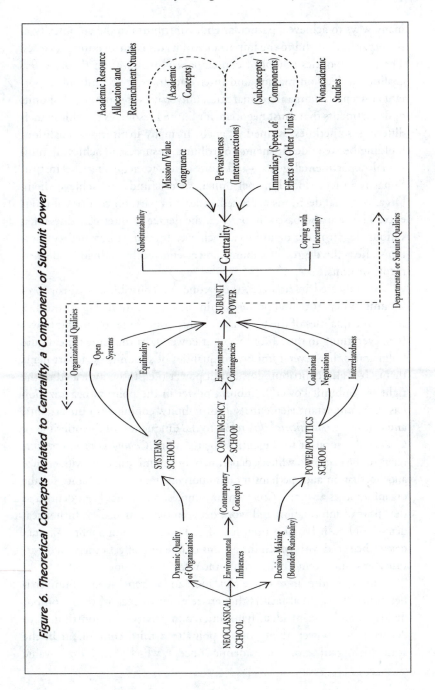

Figure 6. Theoretical Concepts Related to Centrality, a Component of Subunit Power

many ways to achieve a particular end, contributes to the complexity of the organization and to the importance of its decision-making processes. The power/politics school of contemporary organization theory offers coalitional decision-making and interrelatedness to the mix of important concepts. As organized anarchies, universities are composed of units or departments that must negotiate for limited resources to achieve their differing, sometimes competing, goals. In many institutions, coalition-building between departments contributes to success in achieving individual departmental goals—and quite often to acquiring the institutional resources (location, personnel, space, funds) to achieve them. Organizational decisions are based, at least in part, on coalitional influence. They are also based, in part, on the degree of interrelatedness that various departments or units can achieve. Intraorganizational connections affect the degree of subunit power enjoyed by individual departments or units.

As indicated in figure 6, these concepts contribute to theories of subunit or departmental power within the organization. The figure also shows the qualities of the organization that contribute to subunit power (i.e., everything to the left of "Subunit Power"). At the same time, figure 6 illustrates that several important qualities of subunits or departments themselves also contribute to subunit power (i.e., those indicated to the right of "Subunit Power"). Subunit power in the political organization has three important elements: substitutability, coping with uncertainty, and centrality. *Substitutability* refers to the uniqueness of the offerings of a particular subunit to the entire organization. *Coping with uncertainty* refers to the degree to which a department or subunit can cope with change and fluctuation and, perhaps more important, reduce uncertainty for the organization as a whole. *Centrality*, in simplest terms, has been defined as the "flow of information and work between departments."[110] In nonacademic studies, it has also been found to have two components—immediacy (the speed with which the actions of one unit affect others) and pervasiveness (interconnectivity within the total organization).

Finally, studies in resource allocation and retrenchment in universities contribute several factors that are relevant to each of these components. In addition to identifying interconnectivity as a contributor to departmental power, these studies point to a third component in the academic organization, an academic concept, which is mission or value congruence (meaning the degree to which the subunit or department shares the mission and values of the total institution and/or the administration of the university). Manipulation of resources by departments and subjective interpretation of university values or mission lead to difficulty in measuring centrality. Chapter 3 outlines a study designed to overcome these difficulties and develop indicators of centrality for the academic library.

Notes

1. Henry Mintzberg, *Mintzberg on Management* (New York: Free Pr., 1989), 268.

2. Jay M. Shafritz and J. Steven Ott, *Classics of Organization Theory*, 2nd. rev. ed. (Chicago: Dorsey Pr., 1987), 10.

3. Ibid., 21.

4. Herbert A. Simon, "The Proverbs of Administration," *Public Administration Review* 6 (winter 1946): 53–67.

5. R.M. Cyert and James G. March, "A Behavioral Theory of Organizational Objectives," in *Modern Organization Theory*, ed. M. Haire (New York: Wiley, 1959), 76–90; reprinted in Shafritz and Ott, *Classics of Organization Theory*, 155–65. Page numbers for this source and others cited in reprints refer to the reprint edition.

6. Talcott Parsons, "Suggestions for a Sociological Approach to the Theory of Organizations," *Administrative Science Quarterly* 1 (1956): 63–85; reprinted in Shafritz and Ott, *Classics of Organization Theory*, 134.

7. Ludwig von Bertanlanffy, *General System Theory: Foundations, Development, Applications* (New York: G. Braziller, 1968); Norbert Weiner, *Cybernetics* (Cambridge, Mass.: M.I.T. Pr., 1948).

8. Shafritz and Ott, *Classics of Organization Theory*, 234.

9. Helen A. Howard, "Organization Theory and Its Applications in Research in Librarianship," *Library Trends* 22 (spring 1984): 479.

10. William G. Scott, "Organization Theory: A Reassessment," *Academy of Management Journal* 17 (June 1974): 242.

11. Shafritz and Ott, *Classics of Organization Theory*, 238.

12. A.H. Walker and J.W. Lorsch, "Organizational Choice: Product vs. Function," *Harvard Business Review* 46 (Nov./Dec. 1968): 129–38.

13. Paul R. Lawrence and Jay W. Lorsch, "Organization–Environment Interface," in *Developing Organizations: Diagnosis and Action* (Reading, Mass.: Addison-Wesley, 1969); reprinted in Shafritz and Ott, *Classics of Organization Theory*, 204–9.

14. Tom Burns and G.M. Stalker, *The Management of Innovation* (London: Tavistock, 1961).

15. Jay Galbraith, *Designing Complex Organizations* (Reading, Mass.: Academic Pr., 1973).

16. Charles Perrow, "The Short and Glorious History of Organization Theory," in *Creative Organization Theory: A Resourcebook*, ed. Gareth Morgan (Newbury Park, Calif.: 1973), 41–48.

17. R.M. Cyert and James G. March, *A Behavioral Theory of the Firm* (Englewood Cliffs, N.J.: Prentice-Hall, 1963).

18. Shafritz and Ott, *Classics of Organization Theory*, 305.

19. James D. Thompson, *Organizations in Action* (New York: McGraw-Hill), 1967.

20. John P. Kotter, *Power and Influence: Beyond Formal Authority* (New York: Free Pr., 1985). See also Robert W. Allen and Lyman W. Porter, eds., *Organizational Influence Processes* (Glenview, Ill.: Scott, Foresman, 1983).

21. Lowell A. Martin, *Organizational Structure of Libraries* (Metuchen, N.J.: Scarecrow Pr., 1984), 159.

22. W. Boyd Rayward, "Libraries as Organizations," *College & Research Libraries* 30 (July 1969): 316. Although there is a body of literature on the environments (e.g., organizations) that interact with the academic library, this discussion does not address those environments, except as they relate to the university as an organization.

23. J. Victor Baldridge, David V. Curtis, George P. Ecker, and Gary L. Riley, "Alternative Models of Governance in Higher Education," in *Governing Academic Organizations*, eds. J. Victor Baldridge and Terrence Deal (Berkeley, Calif.: McCutchan, 1977): reprinted in *ASHE Reader on Organization and Governance in Higher Education*, 3rd. ed., ed. Marvin W. Peterson (Lexington, Mass.: Ginn Pr., 1986), 12.

24. David A. Garvin, *The Economics of University Behavior* (New York: Academic Pr., 1980), 1.

25. Baldridge et al., "Alternative Models of Governance in Higher Education," 15.

26. Frederick S. Hills and Thomas A. Mahoney, "University Budgets and Organizational Decision-Making," *Administrative Science Quarterly* 23 (Sept. 1978): 454.

27. Jeffrey Pfeffer, "Understanding the Role of Power in Decision-making," *Power in Organizations* (Marshfield, Mass.: Pitman, 1982), 1–32; reprinted in Shafritz and Ott, *Classics of Organization Theory*, 332, figure 1.

28. Dwight R. Ladd, "Myths and Realities of University Governance," *College & Research Libraries* 36 (Mar. 1975): 97.

29. Baldridge et al., "Alternative Models of Governance in Higher Education," 14.

30. There is a considerable body of literature on the characteristics of professionals. Among those characteristics that affect the operation of the university are: demand for autonomy; loyalties to the profession rather than to the

organization; professional values that conflict with "bureaucratic expectations"; and demand for peer evaluation. See Baldridge et al., "Alternative Models of Governance in Higher Education," 13–15.

31. Douglas A.L. Auld, Graham Bannock, R.E. Baxter, and Ray Rees, *The American Dictionary of Economics* (New York: Facts on File, 1983), 28.

32. See, for example, Otto M. Davis, M.A.H. Dempster, and Aaron Wildavsky, "A Theory of the Budgetary Process," *American Political Science Review* 60 (Sept. 1966): 529–47; Gerald R. Salancik and Jeffrey Pfeffer, "The Bases and Uses of Power in Organizational Decision-Making," *Administrative Science Quarterly* 19 (Dec. 1974): 453–73.

33. See Thompson, *Organizations in Action*; Hills and Mahoney, "University Budgets and Organizational Decision-Making," 454.

34. Kent John Chabotar and James P. Honan, "Coping with Retrenchment: Strategies and Tactics," *Change* 22 (Nov./Dec. 1990): 31.

35. Kenneth P. Mortimer and Michael L. Tierney, *The Three "R's" of the Eighties: Reduction, Reallocation, and Retrenchment*, AAHE/Higher Education Research Report No. 4 (Washington, D.C.: American Association for Higher Education, 1979), 29.

36. See Judith Dozier Hackman, "Power and Peripherality: Developing a Practical Theory of Resource Allocations in Colleges and Universities" (Ph.D. diss., University of Michigan, Ann Arbor, 1983) 164; Ellis E. McCune, "Resource Allocation at California State University, Hayward," in "Allocating and Reallocating Financial Resources in an Environment of Fiscal Stress," ed. Robert A. Wilson, Topical Paper No. 24. *Selected Proceedings of the Annual Conference on Higher Education* (Tucson, Ariz.: Univ. of Arizona, 9th Center for the Study of Higher Education, 1984), 26–35. ERIC ED 251 025.

37. Raymond F. Zammuto, "Managing Decline in American Higher Education," in *Higher Education: Handbook of Theory and Research, Vol. II*, ed. John C. Smart (New York: Agathon Pr., 1986), 52.

38. Daniel Katz and Robert L. Kahn, *The Social Psychology of Organizations* (New York: Wiley, 1966).

39. Hills and Mahoney, "University Budgets and Organizational Decision-Making."

40. Paula Choate Baltes, "Toward a Theory of Retrenchment in Higher Education," (Ph.D. diss., University of Arizona, 1985).

41. Fife quoted in Gerlinda S. Melchiori, *Planning for Program Discontinuance: From Default to Design*. AAHE-ERIC/Higher Education Research Report No. 5 (New York: Exxon Education Foundation, Ann Arbor, Mich.: Michigan University, National Institute of Education, 1982); foreword. ERIC ED 224 451.

42. James Hyatt, Carol Hernstadt Shulman, and Aurora S. Santiago, *Strategies for Effective Resource Management* (Washington, D.C.: National Association of College and University Business Officers, 1984).

43. Mortimer and Tierney, *The Three "R's" of the Eighties*.

44. For more analysis of studies of resource allocation and retrenchment in higher education, see Deborah Jeanne Grimes, "Centrality and the Academic Library" (Ph.D. diss., University of Alabama, 1993).

45. Hyatt et al., *Strategies for Effective Resource Management.*

46. Melchiori, *Planning for Program Discontinuance*, 1.

47. See, for example, Melchiori, *Planning for Program Discontinuance*; Yvonna S. Lincoln and Jane Tuttle, "Centrality as a Prior Criterion." Paper presented at the Joint Meeting of the Association for the Study of Higher Education and the American Educational Research Association, Division J, San Francisco, Oct. 19–21, 1983. ERIC ED 240 934; Marianne Cooper and Shoshana Kaufman, "Library Schools and Their Host Academic Libraries: Relationships, Power, Perceptions," *Journal of Academic Librarianship* 16 (Mar. 1990): 27–34.

48. A number of articles suggest that the closings of library schools present a professional crisis. See, for example, the theme issue of *Library Quarterly* 61 (July 1991).

49. Cooper and Kaufman, "Library Schools and Their Host Academic Libraries."

50. Marion Paris, "Library School Closings: Four Case Studies" (Ph.D. diss., Indiana State University, 1986); Karen Feingold Ceppos, "Innovation and Survival in Library Education" (Ph.D. diss., University of California, Berkeley, 1989).

51. Tom Gaughan, "Taking the Pulse of Library Education. Part I," *American Libraries* 22 (Dec. 1991): 1020–21+, and "Part II," *American Libraries* 23 (Jan. 1992): 24–25.

52. See, for example, Mortimer and Tierney, *The Three "R's" of the Eighties*; Melchiori, *Planning for Program Discontinuance*; Hannah Ashar, "Internal and External Variables and Their Effect on a University's Retrenchment Decisions: Two Theoretical Perspetives" (Ph.D. diss., University of Washington, 1987).

53. See, for example, Mortimer and Tierney, *The Three "R's" of the Eighties*; G. Gregory Lozier and P. Richard Althouse, "Supporting Quality through Priority Setting and Reallocation." Paper presented at 22nd. Annual Forum of the Association for Institutional Research, Denver, Colo., May 16–19, 1982. ERIC ED 220 053; C. Stuart Dube II and Albert W. Brown, "Strategic Assessment— A Rational Response to University Cutbacks," *Long-Range Planning* 16 (Apr. 1983): 105–13; Melchiori, *Planning for Program Discontinuance.*

54. See, for example, Mortimer and Tierney, *The Three "R's" of the Eighties*; Dube and Brown, "Strategic Assessment"; Hyatt, Shulman, and Santiago, *Strategies for Effective Resource Management*; Annette Carolyn Caruso, "Implementing Program Review: An Analysis of the Graduate Program Review Process at the Pennsylvania State University from 1971 to 1983". (D.Ed. diss., Pennsylvania State University, 1985).

55. For detailed definitions of power, see David Sils, ed., *International Encyclopedia of the Social Sciences* (New York: Macmillan Co. and Free Pr., 1968); Salancik and Pfeffer, "The Bases and Uses of Power in Organizational Decision-Making"; Allen and Porter, *Organizational Influence Processes*; Hannah Arendt,

On Violence (New York: Harcourt, Brace, Jovanovich, 1970); Edwin Dewey Bell, "Some Theoretical Implications of Power, Resource Allocation, and Theories of Action in Higher Education" (Ed.D. diss., University of North Carolina at Greensboro, 1985); and many others.

56. Shafritz and Ott, *Classics of Organization Theory*, 327.

57. Thomas J. Gavin, "Departmental Budget Allocations and Power in a Community College" (Ph.D. diss., University of Oregon, 1984), 10.

58. Michel Crozier, *The Bureaucratic Phenomenon* (Chicago: Univ. of Chicago Pr., 1964).

59. Perrow, "The Short and Glorious History of Organization Theory," 65.

60. D.J. Hickson, C.R. Hinings, C.A. Lee, R.E. Schneck, and J.M. Pennings, "A 'Strategic Contingencies' Theory of Intraorganizational Power," *Administrative Science Quarterly* 16 (June 1971): 216–29.

61. Ibid. , 219.

62. Crozier, *The Bureaucratic Phenomenon.*

63. Hickson et al., "A 'Strategic Contingencies' Theory of Intraorganizational Power."

64. C.R. Hinings, D.J. Hickson, J.M. Pennings, and R.E. Schneck, "Structural Conditions of Intraorganizational Power," *Administrative Science Quarterly* 19 (Mar. 1974): 40.

65. Keith G. Provan, "Environment, Department Power, and Strategic Decision-Making in Organizations: A Proposed Integration," *Journal of Management* 15 (Mar. 1989): 21–34.

66. Carol S. Saunders and Richard Scamell, "Intraorganizational Distributions of Power: Replication Research," *Academy of Management Journal* 25 (Mar. 1982): 192–200.

67. Bruce J. Fried, "Power Acquisition in a Health Care Setting: An Application of Strategic Contingencies Theory," *Human Relations* 42 (Dec. 1988): 915–27.

68. Iris Cohen and Ran Lachman, "The Generality of the Strategic Contingencies Approach to Subunit Power," *Organization Studies* 9 (Oct. 1988): 371–91.

69. Ran Lachman, "Power from What? A Re-examination of Its Relationships with Structural Conditions," *Administrative Science Quarterly* 34 (June 1989): 231–51.

70. Hills and Mahoney, "University Budgets and Organizational Decision-Making." Hills and Mahoney found "universalistic" criteria used in university budgeting during periods of abundance to include history (previous budgets); fair-share increases (fixed percentage increase across the board); total workload; change in overall workload; student credit hour production (weighted by level of instruction, graduate or undergraduate FTE); and workload efficiency.

71. Jeffrey Pfeffer and Gerald R. Salancik, "Organizational Decision-Making as a Political Process: The Case of the University Budget," *Administrative Science Quarterly* 19 (June 1974): 135–51. A number of subsequent studies

confirmed the findings of Pfeffer and Salancik regarding the effects of sub-unit power in universities. For details, see Salancik and Pfeffer, "The Bases and Uses of Power in Organizational Decision-Making"; Ellen Earle Chaffee, "Decision Models in University Budgeting" (Ph.D. diss., Stanford University, 1981); Abigail Hubbard, "Structural Power and Resource Allocation in the Multicampus University System" (Ph.D. diss., University of Nebraska, Lincoln, 1983).

72. Hackman, "Power and Peripherality"; Ashar, "Internal and External Variables and Their Effect on a University's Retrenchment Decisions."

73. ACRL, College Library Standards Committee, "Standards for University Libraries: Evaluation of Perfomance," *College & Research Libraries News* 30 (Sept. 1989): 344.

74. Hickson et al., "A 'Strategic Contingencies' Theory of Intraorganizational Power," 221.

75. Saunders and Scamell, "Intraorganizational Distributions of Power," 193.

76. Lachman, "Power from What?" 233.

77. Hickson et al., "A 'Strategic Contingencies' Theory of Intraorganizational Power," 221.

78. Sid Huff, "Power and the Information Systems Department," *Business Quarterly* 55 (winter 1991): 51.

79. Hickson et al., "A 'Strategic Contingencies' Theory of Intraorganizational Power," 221–22.

80. Hinings et al., "Structural Conditions of Intraorganizational Power."

81. Crozier, *The Bureaucratic Phenomenon.*

82. Although we might say the same for the systems department within the academic library, we have greater substitutability of actions than some academic units. For example, circulation can be handled manually; online cataloging can be done offline until the system is back online; and unless all resources are in electronic format only, reference assistance depends more on the skills and memory of the reference librarian than on the library computer system.

83. Hickson et al., "A 'Strategic Contingencies' Theory of Intraorganizational Power"; Saunders and Scamell, "Intraorganizational Distribution of Power."

84. Hyatt, Shulman, and Santiago, *Strategies for Effective Resource Management,* 79, 51.

85. Kathleen M. Heim and J. Keith Ostertag, "Sources of Institutional Power: An Analysis of Faculty Policy Participation as an Agent of Influence and Domain," *Library Quarterly* 61 (July 1991): 283.

86. Gaughan, "Taking the Pulse of Library Education, Part II," 25.

87. Herbert S. White, "Politics: The World We Live In," *Library Quarterly* 61 (July 1991): 266.

88. Margaret F. Stieg, "The Closing of Library Schools: Darwinism at the University," *Library Quarterly* 61 (July 1991): 268.

89. Zammuto, "Managing Decline in American Higher Education," 54.

90. Ibid., 58.

91. Chabotar and Honan, "Coping with Retrenchment," 31.

92. Lincoln and Tuttle, *Centrality as a Prior Criterion*, 9.

93. Judith Dozier Hackman, "Power and Centrality in the Allocation of Resources in Colleges and Universities," *Administrative Science Quarterly* 30 (Mar. 1985): 62; see also, Katz and Kahn, *The Social Psychology of Organizations,* and James G. March and Herbert A. Simon, *Organizations* (New York: Wiley, 1958).

94. Hackman, "Power and Peripherality," 7, 9.

95. J. Richard Polidoro, *Rebalancing the University: Will Physical Education Survive?* Kingston, R. I.: University of Rhode Island, 1983. ERIC ED 235 126.

96. Stanley O. Ikenberry and Renee C. Friedman, *Beyond Academic Departments*, 2nd. ed. (San Francisco: Jossey-Bass, 1972).

97. As suggested by Hickson et al., "A 'Strategic Contingencies' Theory of Intraorganizational Power."

98. Richard P. Heydinger, *Using Program Priorities to Make Retrenchment Decisions: The Case of the University of Minnesota.* (Atlanta: Southern Regional Education Board, 1983) 7. ERIC ED 230 119.

99. McCune, "Resource Allocation at California State University, Hayward."

100. White, "Politics: The World We Live In," 266.

101. Stieg, "The Closing of Library Schools," 268. Similar measures were cited by Stefan D. Bloomfield, *Analytical Tools for Budget Reallocation: A Case Study.* Paper presented at 24th Annual Forum of the Association for Institutional Research, Forth Worth, Texas, May 6–9, 1984. ERIC, ED 246 790; Heydinger, *Using Program Priorities Make Retrenchment Decisions*; McCune, "Resource Allocations at California State University, Hayward."

102. Ashar, "Internal and External Variables and Their Effect on a University's Retrenchment Decisions," 48.

103. Ibid.

104. Hanna Ashar and Jonathan Z. Shapiro, "Measuring Centrality: A Note on Hackman's Resource Allocation Theory," *Administrative Science Quarterly* 33 (June 1988): 275–83.

105. Melchiori, *Planning for Program Discontinuance*, 34.

106. Lloyd G. Cooper, "The Politics of Retrenchment in Higher Education." Paper presented at the National Conference of Professors of Educational Administration, San Marcos, Tex., Aug. 15–10, 1982, 6. ERIC, ED 225 500: 6.

107. Paris, "Library School Closings: Four Case Studies."

108. Quoted by Gaughan, "Taking the Pulse of Library Education, Part II," 25.

109. Jeffrey Katzer, "A Lesson to be Learned," *Library Quarterly* 61 (June 1991): 292.

110. Saunders and Scamell, "Intraorganizational Distributions of Power," 193.

3. A Study of Academic Library Centrality

The theory outlined in chapter 2 and the studies on which it is based suggest ways in which centrality may be studied in the academic library. Because Chief Academic Officers (CAOs) and Chief Executive Officers (CEOs) directly influence the most important resource allocations to the academic library, we must know what they think about the library and its services; we must study what academic administrators consider to be relevant indicators of the library's centrality to their institutions. The study described in this chapter was conducted in five American universities to find out just what the university CEO and CAO say about the "heart of the university" metaphor, the mission of the academic library, and specific ways the library demonstrates centrality. The research methodology is described below, as are the five universities that participated in the study. The remainder of the chapter describes the three phases of the research design.

The Research Methodology

The research methodology and design were based primarily on the studies of Jeffrey Pfeffer and Gerald R. Salancik and Judith Dozier Hackman, which use grounded theory methodology.[1] Pfeffer and Salancik studied subunit or departmental power in academic departments and its effects on resource allocation at the University of Illinois at Urbana-

Champaign. They interviewed and surveyed department heads and analyzed university documents to measure workload and participation on
university committees. Using a similar framework, Hackman studied
measures of departmental power, including centrality, in six institutions
of higher education located in the northeastern United States. She, too,
used interviews and document analysis to obtain data from which to
generate theory. Studies in librarianship have employed similar research
techniques. Marion Paris, for example, used case studies and interviews
to gain insight into the closings of four library schools.[2] Jeffrey A. Raffel
and Robert Shishko used the case study technique to develop hypoth-
eses in a cost-benefit analysis of the libraries of the Massachusetts Institute of Technology (M.I.T.).[3] James A. Hyatt and Aurora S. Santiago
conducted case study research on four universities and their libraries to
determine the ways in which libraries cope with the information explosion and related library automation technologies.[4] Larry L. Hardesty
and David Kaser interviewed thirty-nine college administrators regarding their views of the academic library.[5]

The research project described here was a systematic analysis of concepts, definitions, and propositions in order to generate theory. The ultimate goal was to identify "empirical indicators," similar to those identified for academic departmental centrality, that link the concept of academic library centrality with actual experience. Based on the models of
Florence S. Fawcett and Jacqueline Downs,[6] figure 7 illustrates this link.

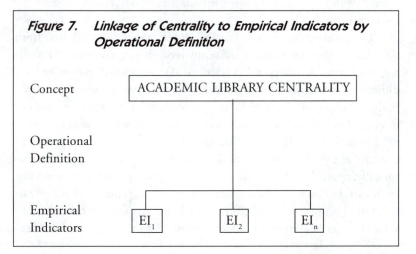

Figure 7.   Linkage of Centrality to Empirical Indicators by Operational Definition

Concept   ACADEMIC LIBRARY CENTRALITY

Operational
Definition

Empirical EI_1 EI_2 EI_n
Indicators

In this figure, centrality is the concept we want to define. We seek empirical indicators; that is, actions or relationships that show how a library is central. Based on what we learn about these indicators, we link the concept, centrality, with its empirical indicators through an operational definition. An operational definition is how the concept is measured. The grounded theory approach focuses on concepts that are drawn from the data rather than from abstract theory. Unlike classical theory, which proposes a theory before searching for facts, grounded theory begins with observable phenomena or facts, then categorizes or groups those facts that have similar characteristics, and finally moves toward theory that explains relationships between the categories. It involves three steps:

1. entering the field work phase without a hypothesis;
2. describing what happens;
3. formulating explanations as to why it happens on the basis of observation.[7]

The grounded theory approach is particularly fruitful when we do not understand a particular relationship or phenomenon but know where to search for clues to better understanding.[8] In this case, the concept of centrality as applied to the academic library is not well understood. There are, however, clues in previous studies and practitioner literature on resource allocation and retrenchment in higher education.[9] From these sources, a "laundry list" (figure 8) of possible indicators of academic library centrality was developed for use in the interview stage of the research project.

The primary advantage of this approach is that concepts arise from the data and the viewpoints of those involved, thereby reducing the probability of error. Although a disadvantage of this approach is that we have difficulty generalizing results to other situations, we are more interested in the "conceptual category" than in individual facts. That is, we are not interested in isolated facts, such as circulation statistics, but in groups or categories of facts that have similar characteristics. Another particular concern of this study was to diminish the effects of the lip service historically applied to the academic library's place within the university. In this study, "lip service" was identified as broad, generalized comments of a lofty nature (such as the intellectual and academic core of the university). Interview questions were structured so that the first one pro-

---

Figure 8.   Possible Indicators of Academic Library Centrality[10]

National prestige

ARL ranking

Acquisition of outside funding

Research or paradigm development by library personnel

Quality of library personnel

Campus visibility (literally and
figuratively)

Service to other units

Use (circulation, interlibrary loan,
etc.)

Innovation/creativity

Program costs

Symbolic vs. practical roles of the
library

Control of critical resources

Connections with other units

Support of specific groups for the
library

Reputation

Comparison to other libraries or
universities

Instructional or research collaborations

Involvement of librarians and/or
the library director in the faculty senate or committee structure

Quality of collections

Participation in high-level decision-making

Substitutability

Proportion of graduates to undergraduates

Relationships with other institutions

Geographic uniqueness

Control of uncertainty

Contributions to university mission

Amount of research conducted in
other units

Faculty or student views of the library

---

vided an opportunity for the participants to make lofty or rhetorical statements, and subsequent questions were designed to probe for more specific information.

Participating Universities

Five public, state-supported universities were included in the study, each offering both graduate and undergraduate instruction and each from a different geographical section of the United States. An attempt was made to include universities that offer a variety of sizes, priorities, and proximities to other libraries or research centers. Interviewees from each institution were assured of anonymity; therefore, participating institutions are identified in the following discussion by number (e.g., University 1 or U1). Further similarities and differences among participating universities are indicated in the descriptions given below. Data for these descriptions were taken from interviews, the *American Library Directory 1989-90*, Fiske's *Comparative Guide to Colleges, American Universities and Colleges*, and memoranda regarding ARL rankings and library expenditures.[11] Specific citations to these sources are not included in order to provide anonymity to participants. The following descriptions are based on the characteristics of the institutions at the time of the study (1992) and may not be totally consistent with today's characteristics.

University 1

U1 was included in the study as an example of a "quintessential large state university."[12] Founded in 1820, U1 is the oldest institution included in the study. It is located in a university town with a population of almost 150,000 in the East South Central region.[13] Also located in the community are a small public library system with three branches, a small historically Black university, a community college, and small state and federal medical facilities that provide libraries. The nearest research collection is a medium-sized medical library located approximately sixty miles away. U1, which offers eight undergraduate programs, is especially strong in arts and sciences and business, and has graduate programs and several professional programs, including law and medicine. It awards bachelor, master's, doctoral, and professional degrees. Its enrollment is almost 20,000 students. U1 falls in the lower 15 percent of the ARL rankings, with a library of 1.8 million volumes and a library budget of almost $7.1 million, or four percent of the total university budget (which is one of the higher percentages of total university budgets among ARL members). In addition to the main library, there are three branches and two separately administered libraries for health sciences and law. U1 is currently involved in a library building program, with a recently completed science library, a business library under construction, and a special collections facility in the design phase. U1 is the largest campus in a three-university system administered by a chancellor. Each university has its own president. At U1, the chief library officer (CLO) is the dean of libraries, who reports to the provost and vice president for academic affairs (who reports to the university president). As such, the dean of libraries participates in university-wide decision-making at the level of other academic deans.

University 2

University 2 is a land-grant university founded in 1857 in a rurally isolated community in the Middle Atlantic region of the United States. The nearest major research library is more than one hundred miles away, and the community's small public library serves a population of approximately 61,000. U2 is included in the study as an example of a very large state university, with an enrollment of almost 40,000 students, with strong programs in agriculture, biological sciences, and business and management. It offers degrees from the associate through the doctoral, including professional degrees in veterinary medicine. As a member of ARL, U2 is ranked in the top 20 percent, offering a collection of 2.3 million volumes through a main library and five departmental/branch libraries, as well as campus libraries located throughout the state at twenty-one sites. Its library budget is approximately $17.2 million, more than two percent of the university's total budget. A science library is under construction. U2 is the main campus of a large state university system with five campuses that offer full degree programs and eighteen campuses that provide courses for the first two years of college. The system is administered under one provost, with each campus managed as a separate organization with its own president and administrative staff. The CLO at U2 is the dean of libraries, who reports to the executive vice president (who reports to the president). The dean of libraries sits on the Council of Academic Deans, whose members follow the same reporting procedures and who participate in university-wide decision-making for academic programs.

University 3

University 3 is a relatively young institution founded in 1961. Although its immediate community is quite small, featuring only a few small special libraries associated with local business or industry, it was included in the study as an example of an urban university located in a resource-rich area, close to other major research libraries or facilities. Located in the Pacific region, U3 offers strong programs in biological sciences and both graduate and undergraduate research programs. Degrees awarded by U3 are bachelor, master's, doctoral, and professional. Most of U3's 15,000 students live off-campus, creating a different environment from that of other universities included in the study. Its library serves many users not enrolled in the university. U3 is ranked in ARL's lower 30 percent, with a collection of almost 1.4 million volumes, resulting from rapid growth during the late 1960s and early 1970s. Its library budget of approximately $11.3 million is slightly over three percent of the university's total budget, despite its being the smallest university in the study. U3 has four branch or departmental libraries, with a science library facility under construction. U3 is part of a large state university system administered by one president, with each university managed as a separate organization by a chancellor. The director of libraries is considered by the chancellor to be "essentially the equivalent of a dean", (quoted from research interview), serving as a member of the executive program and reporting to the vice chancellor for academic affairs (a newly created position; formerly, the director reported to the executive vice chancellor). Despite the characterization of the director of libraries by the chancellor as "essentially the equivalent of a dean," the academic deans report directly to the executive vice chancellor, as does the vice chancellor for academic affairs. The executive vice chancellor reports to the chancellor.

University 4
Founded in 1868, U4 is also a land-grant university located in a geographically isolated section of a state in the North East Central region. It was included in the study because it is touted as "ranking among the world's great universities," with a library that has historically been rated among the top three U.S. academic libraries since its beginnings.[14] U4's immediate community is rurally isolated, offering no other research facilities. The community's small public library system serves a population of less than 100,000. In addition to having the typically strong programs of land-grant universities in agriculture and engineering, it also has strong programs in liberal and performing arts. In fact, twenty of its programs are ranked among the top ten in the United States. Degrees awarded by U4 are bachelor, master's, doctoral, and some professional. Rated in the top five percent of the ARL rankings, U4's library offers 7.5 million volumes to more than 36,000 students through a main library, an undergraduate library, and thirty-eight departmental/ branch libraries, including law and medical libraries. Its budget is approximately $18.5 million, or almost three percent of the total university budget. A science library is under construction. U4 is one university in a two-campus state

system administered by one president, with each campus managed independently by its own chancellor. Its CLO is the university librarian, who reports to the vice chancellor (who reports to the chancellor) and who participates in decision-making as a member of the Council of Deans.

University 5

University 5 was also included in the study as an example of a university located less than one hundred miles from other major research libraries or facilities. It is a state university, located in the South Atlantic region of the United States, with an enrollment of more than 21,000 students. U5 was founded in 1968 by consolidating two older institutions of higher education. Its primary strengths are its programs in biomedical research, with the majority of students enrolled in junior- and senior-level classes. U5 offers associate, bachelor, master's, and doctoral degrees through two campuses situated only a few miles apart. Located in the state capital, U5 is near information and research centers associated with state government as well as with state historical associations. In addition, the city of more than 800,000 offers a small university with a law school, a community college, and a public library system with eight branches. U5 is not a member of ARL. Its library collection is approximately 743,000 volumes; its library budget is approximately $7.1 million, or one percent of the total university budget. The state funding system was recently restructured so that U5 receives library funding on the same level as other research institutions in the state (formerly defined by the state legislature as membership in ARL). According to the CEO, the infusion of new funds will be used in collection development, especially for the acquisition of databases, in the area of health sciences. The CLO is the director of university library services/university librarian, who reports to the provost/vice president for academic affairs (who reports to the president). The director sits on the Council of Deans, the council of university Administrators, and the University Assembly (which consists of faculty, administrators, and students). The library budget is submitted through the Executive Budget Committee to the President's Council.

Summary of University Descriptions

In summary, the participating universities ranged in enrollment size from

15,000 to almost 40,000. The following geographical regions of the United States were represented: East South Central, Middle Atlantic, Pacific, North East Central, and South Atlantic. Of the four universities that hold membership in ARL, rankings varied from the top five percent to the lower 15 percent. Library collection sizes ranged from less than one million volumes to 7.5 million volumes, with library budgets ranging from $7 million to more than $18 million, and percentages of university budgets ranging from a low of one percent to a high of four percent. All universities were public, state-supported institutions. One is located in a large, urban resource-rich environment; one is located quite near a major U. S. research center; the remaining three are geographically isolated from other research centers. Although each university offered a full range of undergraduate and graduate programs, the strengths varied from agriculture to liberal arts to business to biomedical research. The administrative structures were primarily the same, with titles varying slightly, but with the CLO reporting to the CAO on each campus. On one campus, the CLO reported one administrative step below that of academic deans. In all, considerable diversity was exhibited among the project participants. This summary of characteristics is also presented in table form in table 1.

Research Design
Phase One: Literature Review
The first phase of the study was a review of relevant literature of organization theory, especially in the areas of resource allocation and retrenchment in higher education. Important concepts from these areas are relevant to the study of academic library centrality. Therefore, the purpose of this phase was to examine and clarify the concepts of resource allocation, retrenchment, power, and, finally, centrality. In addition, the literature was examined to identify possible indicators of centrality for the academic library, along the lines of measures of centrality identified for academic departments by Hills and Mahoney, Pfeffer and Salancik, Hackman, and Ashar.[15] Some subunit indicators of centrality identified in these studies were assumed to be appropriate to the academic library's position within the university (e.g., administrative service to the university); however, other indicators were expected to be inappropriate (e.g., credit hour production).

Table 1. Summary of Characteristics of Universities Participating in the Study

University	Year Founded	Enrollment Awarded	Degrees	Major Programs	Distance to Nearest Research Library	Title of CLO	Officer to Whom CLO Reports	% University Budget for Library Resources	Collection Size
Pilot 1	1966	16,000	Bachelor's Master's Doctorate Professional	Medical and health sciences, business	60 miles	(2) Director of Libraries	(1) VP for Academic Affairs (1) VP for Medical Affairs	<1.0	1.1 million volumes
Pilot 2	1963	>9,000	Associate Bachelor's Master's Doctorate Professional	Business and managemt.	60 miles	Dean of Libraries	Provost/VP for Academic Affairs	3.0	365,000 volumes
U1	1820	20,000	Bachelor's Master's Doctorate Professional	Arts and sciences; business	60 miles	Dean of Libraries	Provost/VP for Academic Affairs	4.0	1.8 million volumes
U2	1857	40,000	Associate Bachelor's Master's Doctorate Professional	Agriculture, biological sciences, business	100+ miles	Dean of Libraries	Executive VP	2.0+	2.3 million volumes
U3	1961	15,000	Bachelor's Master's Doctorate Professional	Biological sciences	Same city	Dean of Libraries	Vice Chancellor for Academic Affairs	3.0+	1.4 million volumes
U4	1868	36,000	Bachelor's Master's Doctorate Professional	Agriculture; engineering	100 miles	University Librarian	Vice Chancellor	<3.0	7.5 million volumes
U5	1968	21,000	Associate Bachelor's Master's Doctorate Professional	Biomedical research	>100 miles	Director of Library Services/ University Librarian	Provost/VP for Academic Affairs	1.0	743,000 volumes

Phase Two: Pilot Study

In the second phase of research, a pilot study of semistructured interviews was conducted, with interview questions focused on four major areas of concern:

　　1. The connection between the "heart of the university" metaphor and the university library's mission;

　　2. Refinement of the definition of centrality;

　　3. The contributions of the university library to the university's mission and immediate priorities;

　　4. Possible indicators of academic library centrality.

Testing and revision of the interview format was conducted prior to its use at the five designated universities through interviews with two CAOs in two state universities. Descriptions of the two universities participating in the pilot interview are given below because results of the pilot interviews are included with those of the formal study. The universities involved in the pilot study are designated by number (e.g., Pilot 1 and Pilot 2). Both pilot universities are part of the same state system in the East South Central region of the United States; neither pilot university is a member of ARL. Both are located in urban areas where there are strong scientific or technical interests.

Pilot 1, founded in 1966, has a student population of almost 16,000, enrolled primarily in medical and health sciences programs and in business programs, with enrollment in other fields beginning to increase. Pilot 1 awards the bachelor's, master's, doctoral, and professional degrees. It is strongly tied to the medical and research programs of its immediate community; in fact, its service mission tends to be directed locally rather than statewide. Pilot 1's library has a collection of 1.1 million volumes and a budget of more than $1.8 million, or well under one percent of its institutional budget of $736.5 million. The library includes two main facilities, one designated as the medical library and the other as the academic library, with one branch library. Pilot 1 is located in the largest metropolitan area in the state in a community that also hosts a public library system serving a population of more than 280,000, two other four-year colleges, two other two-year colleges, numerous small scientific and technical libraries, and several small medical or hospital libraries. Pilot 1 is one of three universities in a state system under the administration of one chancellor. The two main libraries are managed by directors, who hold the equivalent of the position of academic dean; one reports directly to the vice president for academic affairs, and the other reports directly to the vice president for medical affairs. Both vice presidents report to the president of the university. The library directors participate in weekly deans' meetings and function at the same level of university administration as the academic deans.

As part of the same state system, Pilot 2 is also managed by the university president. However, its internal organizational structure is somewhat different. Its CLO is the dean of libraries (recently changed from director), who reports to the provost/vice president for academic affairs. The dean of libraries sits on the Council of Academic Officers, which includes the academic deans, associate vice presidents, and the associate provost. At this level, the dean of libraries is involved in institutionwide decisions regarding strategic planning and budget. Pilot 2 was founded in 1963 in a rapidly growing scientific and technical community of almost 150,000. Its program emphases, however, lie in business and management. Pilot 2 awards degrees from the associate through the doctorate as well as a few professional degrees. Much smaller than Pilot 1, its enrollment is less than 9,000. The library of Pilot 2 includes approximately 365,000 volumes, with a budget of more than $1.4 million, or approximately three percent of the total university budget. Also served by the community are a small historically Black college, a large public library system, and a large multitype library system extending to several surrounding counties. Both universities are representative of typical state universities with different histories and program emphases. They are not unlike the institutions selected for the formal research phase of the project.

Phase Three: Formal Interviews

The third phase of the research design consisted of formal interviews with the CAO and CEO at each of the participating universities. As suggested previously, these individuals are the primary decision makers on each campus, and some of their decisions are based on the centrality of a program or department to the university's mission. Consequently, their views are quite relevant to the concept of centrality as applied to the academic library in relation to the university's mission. Although the use of individual interviews may suggest the *micro*analytic study, the focus of the interview questions was on the *macro*analytic unit of the university and not on the behavior of the individual interviewees.

Face-to-face interviews, rather than telephone interviews, were used to give the researcher direct contact with the interviewee, to ensure that adequate time was given for the interview (without the distractions or rescheduling that may occur with telephone interviews), and to allow the researcher to visit each campus and collect additional information through observation or document analysis. The purpose of this phase was to gather information in order to refine the concept of academic library centrality and to expand the range of possible indicators of academic library centrality, confirming some and rejecting others found relevant to academic departments. Because of the differences in functions between the academic department and the academic library, the researcher expected to identify additional indicators in this phase that are unique to the academic library.

Summary

Based on a review of the methodology employed in similar studies, this research project followed a modified grounded theory methodology in which theory is embedded in the actual findings of the study. This approach was particularly appropriate because parts of the phenomenon of academic library centrality are not yet well known, but previous theory and research provide important clues. Although there are weaknesses in the use of grounded theory methodology, it has been used quite successfully to generate conceptual categories from facts, which was the intent of this study. More specifically, the purpose of this study was to generate theory in which concepts, definitions, and propositions are systematically examined. The goal was to identify empirical indicators to link the concept of academic library centrality with actual library experience.

Phase one of the study was an intensive literature review, reported in chapter 2, to clarify and distill relevant concepts—resource allocation, retrenchment, subunit power, and centrality—as well as possible indicators of academic library centrality. Using the university as the unit of analysis, phase two was a pilot study to test the interview design in two universities. Phase three included formal interviews with the CEOs and CAOs of five universities. The next chapter examines their responses to the interview questions.

Notes

1. Jeffrey Pfeffer and Gerald R. Salancik, "Organizational Decision-Making as a Political Process: The Case of the University Budget," *Administrative Science Quarterly* 19 (June 1974): 135–51; Salancik and Pfeffer, "The Bases and Uses of Power in Organizational Decision-Making: The Case of the University," *Administrative Science Quarterly* 19 (Dec. 1974): 453–73; Judith Dozier Hackman, "Power and Centrality in the Allocation of Resources in Colleges and Universities," *Administrative Science Quarterly* 30 (Mar. 1985): 61–77.

2. Marion Paris, "Library School Closings: Four Case Studies" (Ph.D. diss., Indiana University, 1986).

3. Jeffrey A. Raffel and Robert Shishko, *Systematic Analysis of University Libraries: An Application of Cost-Benefit Analysis for the M.I.T. Libraries* (Cambridge, Mass.: M.I.T. Pr., 1969).

4. James A. Hyatt and Aurora S. Santiago, *University Libraries in Transition* (Washington, D.C.: National Association of College and University Business Officers, 1987).

5. Larry L. Hardesty and David Kaser, "What Do Academic Administrators Think about the Library?" A Summary Report to the Council on Library Resources. (Grant CLR 8019-A, Feb. 1990, photocopy).

6. Jacqueline Fawcett and Florence S. Downs, *The Relationship of Theory and Research* (Norwalk, Conn.: Appleton-Century-Crofts, 1986).

7. Kenneth D. Bailey, *Methods of Social Research*, 3rd. ed. (New York: Free Pr., 1987), 54.

8. Matthew B. Miles and A. Michael Huberman, *Qualitative Data Analysis: A Sourcebook of New Methods* (Beverly Hills, Calif.: Sage, 1984): 27–28.

9. A detailed description is included in chapter 2. See also Hardesty and Kaser, "What Do Academic Administrators Think about the Library?"; Judith Dozier Hackman, "Power and Peripherality: Developing a Practical Theory of Resources Allocation in Colleges and Universities" (Ph.D. diss., University of Michigan, Ann Arbor, 1983); Frederick S. Hills and Thomas A. Mahoney, "University Budgets and Organizational Decision-Making," *Administrative Science Quarterly* 23 (Sept. 1978): 454–65; Pfeffer and Salancik, "Organizational Decision-Making as a Political Process"; Hanna Ashar, "Internal and External Variables and Their Effect on a University's Retrenchment Decisions: Two Theoretical Perspectives" (Ph.D. diss., University of Washington, 1987).

10. For specific citations to these indicators, see Deborah Jeanne Grimes, "Centrality and the Academic Library" (Ph.D. diss., University of Alabama, 1993).

11. *American Library Directory 1989–90*, 42nd. ed. (Chicago: ALA, 1989); Edward B. Fiske, *Selective Guide to Colleges*, 3rd. ed. (New York: Times Books, 1985); *American Universities and Colleges*, 134th. ed. (New York: Bowker, 1989); Sara M. Pritchard, memoranda to directors of ARL libraries, Apr. 22, 1991; Jan. 21, 1992. ARL rankings are based on a formula that takes into account five variables: number of volumes held; gross number of volumes added; number of

current serials; amount of total expenditures; and total number of professional and nonprofessional staff.

12. Fiske, *Selective Guide to Colleges*.

13. Designations of geographical locations are based on those used by the Association of Research Libraries; see Pritchard, memoranda.

14. Fiske, *Selective Guide to Colleges*.

15. Hills and Mahoney, "University Budgets and Organizational Decision-Making"; Pfeffer and Salancik, "Organizational Decision-Making as a Political Process"; Hackman, "Power and Peripherality"; Ashar, "Internal and External Variables and Their Effect on a University's Retrenchment Decisions."

4. What University Administrators Say about Centrality

Many decisions and actions of librarians are based on assumptions of what university administrators value about both libraries and librarians. Assumptions, however, are not always accurate, and as Larry L. Hardesty and David Kaser observed, "Library directors need to know with some certitude what administrators think about the library."[1] The study outlined in the preceding chapter was an attempt to give academic librarians some certainty by finding out how a group of leading university administrators would respond to specific questions about the academic library and its role on campus. This chapter considers the transcribed comments of the CEOs and CAOs at the seven universities that participated in the pilot and formal studies described in chapter 3. Although research studies do not usually report the results of pilot studies and interview wrap-up questions, the information from both was either very consistent with the results of the formal study or unexpectedly telling; therefore, these results are included as well. This chapter begins by describing the characteristics of the administrators who participated in the studies and then discusses their responses to the major interview questions and the wrap-up questions.

The Interviewees

The CAO of each university participating in the pilot study and the CEO and CAO of each university participating in the formal study were interviewed at length. With the university as the unit of analysis, diverse institutions with specific characteristics were included. For example, some institutions were chosen because of their proximity to research centers, and others were chosen because of geographic isolation. Some were selected because of a high ARL ranking, and others were chosen because they had a low ARL ranking or no ranking at all. In addition, geographic distribution throughout the United States was a factor in selection. Each university officer was considered an attribute of the university under study rather than an individual subject under study. Descriptive information about each administrator was gathered at the beginning of the interview, including: number of years in present position; number of different positions held in higher education (including faculty positions); number of different universities in which these positions had been held; and field of expertise or research.

The interviewees averaged 3.71 years in their present positions, within a range of one to nine years; they averaged 6.75 different positions in higher education, within a range of four to fifteen positions; and they had been employed, on average, in 3.17 different institutions in their careers, within a range of one to five institutions. They came from diverse fields of expertise: three from history; three from biological sciences; and one each from English, psychology, physics, mechanical engineering, political science, and education. All twelve interviewees were male, held the Ph.D. as the highest earned degree, and were over fifty years of age. Given the nature and history of academia, these similarities were expected. By coincidence, two of the CEOs had previously served as CAOs at other institutions involved in the study. Since the study, at least two of the participants have moved to higher administrative positions within their state university systems. Table 2 provides a summary of the characteristics of the administrators who participated in the interviews.

The Interview Questions

Question 1: What does the phrase "The library is the heart of the university" mean, if anything, to you?

Table 2. Summary of Characteristics of Interviewees

University	Title*	Yrs. in Present Position	No. of Different Positions	No. of Univ. Where Employed	Field of Study
Pilot 1	CAO	1.5	7	3	History
Pilot 2	CAO	2	7	2	Physics
U1	CEO	4	15	+1	Natural Sciences (Genetics/Biology)
U1	CAO	2	6	4	English
U2	CEO	2	10	4	Biology
U2	CAO	1	+4	5	Mechanical Engineering
U3	CEO	9	6	+3	Political Science
U3	CAO	2	4	5	Biological Sciences
U4	CEO	5	7	1	Psychology
U4	CAO	6	6	2	History
U5	CEO	3	4	+6	History
U5	CAO	7	5	2	Education
Range/All		1–9	4–15	1–5	
Averages		3.7	16.75	2.83	

* CAO = e.g., Vice President for Academic Affairs, Provost, Vice Chancellor; CEO = e.g., President, Chancellor
+ Interviewee did not give exact number.

The initial interview question allowed each participant to react to the well-known metaphor. Once the initial question was asked, subquestions or prompts moved the interviewees to more specific responses. As anticipated, university administrators made lofty, rhetorical statements in response to the first question. Using phrases such as "heart of the enterprise [of communicating the university's information to the community] and "intellectual and academic core" to describe the meaning of the metaphor. Most interviewees identified the library as a repository of the accumulated knowledge of humankind and as a "central tool" for the facilitation of the university's mission. Three administrators commented that the university cannot exist without the library because "virtually every enterprise [the university undertakes] requires an excellent library collection and excellent library services" and because, unlike lab supplies or other instructional materials, "it is virtually impossible" to fill a void left by poor funding for library collection development.

Two administrators, however, disagreed with the metaphor, stating that the faculty and students are the heart of the university. When asked to give another conceptualization of the library, however, neither suggested a specific metaphor or description of the library's organizational role. Both used the adjectives "central" and "core" in describing the library's role on campus. Three others stated that the metaphor is more an exaggeration of the library's mission than an actual indication of the various functions the library should fulfill within the university. In these cases, the interviewees emphasized the role of information, rather than the role of the library itself, as essential to the fulfillment of the university's mission. Some interviewees commented on the effects of technology on access to information, suggesting that "how information is organized [whether it is through libraries or via technologies] is immaterial." One administrator did not view the metaphor as equivalent to the library's mission. He stated that technology's role is becoming more significant in the delivery of information to the academic community. He emphasized the library's role in developing technological access to information in the following statement:

> The mission of the library is obviously to develop the capability of tapping the information that is absolutely necessary to the students and faculty to help them get the best education possible and to help them give the best education possible.

In many cases, the question generated a discussion of the debate over access and ownership of information, which is described in more detail under question 2.

Even those interviewees who did not view the metaphor as the equivalent of the mission were quite articulate in their description of the symbolic role of the academic library. Many administrators suggested that the symbolic role of the library relates to both its intellectual mission and its physical reality on campus. One observation was that "the symbolic role [of the academic library] is always important because it says something about the whole university." The following statement exemplifies the symbolic role suggested by interviewees: "The library is the most significant laboratory for the entire university."

When asked if the symbolic role gives the academic library protected status in resource allocation, interviewees cited evidence of the library being "championed by the faculty, championed by the community" or of student willingness to earmark tuition increases for library improvements. One administrator observed: "I think the library's being well taken care of [during resource allocation] reflects a symbolic role, in terms of being a central function."

Most of the interviewees stated that the library is the last unit to receive budget cuts and that it generally receives fewer cuts than other institutional units. These comments beg the questions, Is this true? Is the library budget actually protected, or is this simply oratory? In research studies such as this, the integrity of people who hold high administrative positions must be assumed. There is no way to know, without having been involved in campus discussions, if there was indeed a protection of library interests during resource allocation decisions. However, a review of ACRL and ARL statistics for the years immediately before and after the interviews indicates an increase in total library expenditures per student for each institution in the formal study. In one case, the increase was matched by a decrease in staffing. Although there appears to be an upward funding trend beginning about 1990, percentages of university budgets allocated for library expenditures remain below national library standards. (Additional comments on this topic are included in chapter 5.)

Most interviewees commented that the campus library is a large and imposing edifice situated in a central location. The physical symbolism attributed to the campus library by interviewees is particularly interesting: Four of the five universities in the formal study have recently built, or are currently building, a new science library to serve a cluster of programs and colleges (e.g., biological sciences, agricultural sciences, physics and engineering, medical sciences, etc.). In each case, the administrators observed that there has been considerable campus debate over the physical placement of the new library facility. One interviewee commented:

If you look out of the window, you'll see the new science library. It's centered in an area that is accessible to the college of
medicine, biological sciences, physical sciences, engineering. It
will probably be the most striking and largest building in the
whole area. It'll be a center. It'll be a center for faculty and
students. It has both a physical and intellectual position at the
center of academic endeavors.

In addition, several interviewees suggested that the importance attached to the library as a facility where students can meet and study
reflects its symbolic role on campus. In many cases, the interviewees
lamented the lack of study space as a major weakness of their campus
libraries.

One university library has a long history as an outstanding research
facility. On this campus, the CAO and the CEO agreed that the library's
symbolic role is extremely important, more so than was evident on any
other campus in the study. The CEO observed:

The library holds a very special and privileged place that's not
true in probably most other institutions . . . . We're highly unusual [due to the history of the university and early development of its library collection]. It really has been the corner-
stone of our intellectual growth.

Both men indicated that faculty, in particular, would view the loss
of even one position in the ARL ranking as a "measurable indication
that the quality of the library [has] fallen" and that the university as a
whole is "running downhill and deteriorating." The CAO added:

Although some decline would be seen as a catastrophe, the symbolic [decline] . . . would have a measurable impact on morale,
retention, faculty recruitment.

In addition, the library on this campus is a source of considerable alumni
support and the recipient of extremely large financial gifts.

During further discussion, interviewees weighed the relative importance of the practical and symbolic roles of the university library. In

most cases, they viewed the practical role as more important, suggesting that the library's "functional role gives it protected status." Interestingly, those who favored the practical role cited their professional backgrounds (primarily scientific) as reasons for their emphasis on the practical role of the library. One notable exception is the university library cited in the previous paragraph, where the symbolic role outweighs the practical role.

Although comments on question 1 generally reflect the findings of earlier studies in which college administrators maintain a belief in the symbolic role played by the campus library,[2] some interviewees suggested that the symbolic role of the academic library is changing, influenced by information and telecommunications technologies. They stated, for example, that "the days of great comprehensive libraries are gone." One CEO put it this way:

> I think the symbolic role of the library will diminish with time because the symbolic role is tied generally to a particular edifice, to a building which is usually at the center of campus, and the symbolism is the image of this building where books are stored, where one goes to get knowledge . . . . But the symbolism of access to data and information will grow. There will be a broadening of the image of the library concept. I don't think that protected status will diminish any as the symbolism broadens from edifice to access to information.

To sum up the responses to question 1, university administrators stated that the mission of the academic library is not equivalent to the "heart of the university" metaphor; that the symbolic role of the library, both intellectually and physically, reflects its centrality to the university; and that the library's practical role is more important than its symbolic role.

Question 2: Some institutions define centrality in terms of contributions to the university's mission and some in terms of connections between units. Which would you use?

The second major interview question narrowed the discussion to the two major views of university centrality that emerge from research literature (as discussed in chapter 2). Because the issue of access versus

ownership is often cited in relation to the most critical services and resources offered by the academic library, related comments are included
in the following discussion. Three administrators were uncomfortable
with choosing a specific definition of centrality. They suggested that the
concept is so submerged in their definitions of the university library that
they cannot articulate it separately. For example, one interviewee commented that "the library is so central that it's taken for granted, that it's
not even argued about. It's not a problem I've worried about." In fact,
two interviewees refused to accept either definition or to elaborate on a
definition. The majority, however, applied both definitions of centrality
to the academic library, citing its important role in all aspects of university life. As one CEO observed:

> Both have to obtain for centrality . . . . [T]o have centrality
> in terms of mission, you would really have to have connec-
> tions.

When asked if one aspect of the definition is more important than
the other, most of the interviewees preferred the definition of contributions to the university's mission. They stated, for example:

> I guess if I had to make a choice there, I'd say contributions to
> the mission. I can't ever see us in a situation where the li-
> brary, whatever its conformation, whatever its form, what-
> ever its structure, wherever it's located, its ability to help
> people evaluate different kinds of information wouldn't be
> absolutely necessary.

Another administrator cited the rather specific mission of his institution as his reason for emphasizing connectedness:

> Our interconnections, our centrality of communication
> [throughout the university] is what gives us our centrality of
> mission.

He further observed that his view of centrality is based on the quality of services offered by an academic unit:

I think the quality of your work—when someone comes to you with a need and you can meet that need quickly and effectively—that's what gives you your centrality. People need you, they know you are going to produce, they know you are going to respond, then you become a key player or unit.

Similarly, another CAO said that his rule of thumb regarding centrality is "how many folks will be standing at [my office] door hollerin'—the longer the line, the more the centrality . . . . Centrality is getting information to people who live in information jobs," whatever the means of delivery may be.

Only one institution in the study has a formal written resource allocation plan. It incorporates both major views into a circular definition of centrality as a criterion for program review: How central is the unit to the mission of the campus; internal relationships?

Both the CEO and the CAO of this institution, however, were quite specific in their views of library centrality and the most critical resources and services provided by their library. One of these administrators elaborated on the university's program review criteria, suggesting that the definition of centrality incorporates three other concepts: the population served by the unit; the importance of one unit to others (i.e., will another unit have to assume additional responsibilities if one is eliminated?); and the uniqueness of the unit to outside agencies (e.g., teaching programs or special collections unique to the state or region).

Other administrators suggested a variety of "critical resources" provided by the campus library, including an emphasis on service or "service attitude," storage and retrieval of information, expertise in collection development, instruction to students in use of new information technologies, provision of study space (especially for undergraduates), and "leading-edge" information found in periodicals. One administrator observed that some students "consider their experience in the library as even more important than their experience in the classroom." He also noted that he believes that the age of access should not "undermine the importance of acquisition" and that "libraries will maintain, in spite of all the technological developments, some centrality to the university."

The access/ownership issue appeared frequently during the interviews, often in response to question 2. One CEO stated:

> I think the main thing the library has to provide . . . is access to the widest variety of periodicals and books, reference services—convenience.

All the interviewees observed that no institution can expect to keep pace with the information explosion. Some lamented the loss of the comprehensiveness of their library's collections whereas others, at younger institutions in particular, welcomed the arrival of technologies that reduce the need for collection-building. One administrator suggested that the financial and physical constraints imposed on libraries by the information explosion have significantly increased the need to emphasize access rather than collection-building. Although another CAO does not consider himself a "diehard" over ownership, he stated:

> I'm in this job for a few years, and I'm not going to let the library suffer during my watch.

Others suggested that "the library is a means to an end rather than an end in itself" and that the "mechanism" for providing resources is more important than owning resources. Yet almost every interviewee provided the unsolicited information, with an air of pride, that his university's library is a net lender rather than a net borrower. Administrators also mentioned "quick" or "speedy" access to information frequently. For example, one interviewee stated:

> If the library provided me with information I wanted as quickly as I could get it, as cheaply as possible, then I would say they were fulfilling their major function.

Finally, in response to question 2, university administrators suggested alternatives or substitutions that faculty or students can use to gain information without using the campus library. Two interviewees noted that some faculty members write costs for databases and journal subscriptions into grant proposals to fulfill their information needs directly. One CEO observed:

> If I'm a student who needs to hop on a [database] that I can get in my department but I can't get in my library, then in my own mind the library will not be central to my needs.

Alluding to a previous comment on quality, another administrator stated:

> If they [the students] know you're not going to respond, they don't have any confidence in the quality of what you do. They'll forget you and just move off and do something else. They'll go around you.

Others, however, suggested that the availability of alternative information technologies increases the need for the campus library to serve as a facilitator or coordinator of information technologies and for librarians to play a major role in developing institutional information systems.

The majority viewpoints, then, of administrators of issues raised in question 2 are that (1) both definitions of academic unit centrality found in the literature (e.g., contribution to the institutional mission and connectedness between units) are applicable to academic library centrality; and (2) access to resources, either owned or through other sources, and service related to that access are the most critical contributions of the academic library to the university.

Question 3: Given that the mission of the university is teaching, research, and service, in what ways does the library contribute most to the fulfillment of the university mission?

Question 3 focused on specific ways in which the academic library contributes to the mission of the university. It addressed the current priorities of the university and specific ways in which the library helps the university meet those priorities. The traditionally accepted mission components of teaching, research, and service provided a basis for discussion in question 3. Unfortunately, several administrators gave ambiguous, noncommittal responses to the third question. The prompt "Under what conditions do library matters become a top priority or emergency?" encouraged more specific answers.

Most of the interviewees seemed reluctant to indicate a priority among the three components of the university mission. When pressed, the majority suggested that the traditional order—teaching, research, service—reflected their institutional priorities. The administrators at the two land-grant universities were careful to point out that, particularly in the area of agriculture, public service is an important component of the university mission. Similarly, an administrator at a younger institution remarked that its public service mission is assuming more importance as the institution grows. At another university, both administrators added patient care to the formal mission of their university. Only one interviewee named research as the highest priority at his institution, followed by teaching, then service.

Several interviewees explained the difference between long-term and short-term institutional goals and mission priorities. One CAO stated:

> I see our mission as a general overarching concept. Our priorities are more mutable, more expressive, shorter-term elaborations of the mission. What changes are our goals within the broader mission.

The CEO at the same institution described mission in both philosophical and functional terms. The latter, he said, refers to specific ways the library fulfills its philosophical role. At another institution, the CAO responded:

> The [formal] mission statement doesn't give priorities . . . . If you look at the whole university and how we spend our money and how we make decisions, then teaching comes up as the highest priority, and it probably requires more expensive and varied support.

Regarding the library's contribution to teaching, he noted that the current library facility is overcrowded and too small for the undergraduate population it serves. The university made a special request to the state legislature for library expansion. One CEO explained that teaching research and service are equal at the university level but "unequal as you move into the departments."

Despite a reluctance to give priorities, most interviewees were willing to elaborate on the library's relationship to each of the mission components. For example, one administrator observed that because the library at his institution does not yet "measure up to the standards of a research university," more attention must be given to library development. Because of changes in state funding patterns, another institution has received a 15 percent increase in library funding. The CEO at this institution indicated that 85 percent of the research budget is in health sciences programs; as a result, he suggested that the increases in the library's budget focus on improving the research collections in health sciences. Another interviewee stated:

> I think the library becomes increasingly important as the number of graduate students increases, almost by definition.

Several interviewees agreed with this view, suggesting that the growth of graduate programs "affects the way [resources are allocated] in the library" and "causes considerable concern for the role of the library in providing resources." One CEO replied that he does not believe that the proportion of graduate students to undergraduate students affects the centrality of the library; instead, he believes that it affects the scope and depth of the library collection. When asked about the high level of research conducted at his institution, another administrator observed that "the centrality of being able to obtain data would be greater" than if the research level was low. He further explained:

> That doesn't mean we have to store the information, but we have to be able to tap it.

The CEO at one institution commented that the library is especially important to the development of graduate research specialties. He also noted that undergraduates have different library needs and are generally concerned only that the library is "warm and open when they want to get their books." On the other hand, another administrator responded:

> It's a high priority to retain our strength as a research institution, and the library plays an important role in that. It's a high priority to retain the strength of our undergraduate program, and the library helps in that.

More specifically, the improvement of undergraduate instruction is an important goal at his institution, which had the only written resource allocation plan in this study. The plan directly mentions the library's role in helping to achieve this short-term goal. For example, the plan links institutional emphasis on writing with institutional emphasis on library research for undergraduates. As a result, the writing center was placed in the undergraduate library. Separate from the research library, it provides more study space "to render it more accessible to undergraduates." At a different university, a campus publication indicated that the improvement of undergraduate education has been designated a priority. When asked for specific examples of ways in which this university is going to improve undergraduate education, the CAO gave no answers related to library services or resources. In fact, he simply shrugged off questions about library contributions to this priority.

Two interviewees commented on the high priority placed on the library by faculty members, particularly regarding their research needs. A high priority for the library is important to one university's planning advisory committee: It is a "reflection of the priority given the library by the president." A few interviewees did not believe that the priorities of the university influence the centrality of the library. One administrator stated:

> The centrality is already there. If it were just a research institution, the library would still have centrality. If it were just a teaching institution, the library would still have centrality. . . . [It was exempted as much as possible from reallocation of funds because] it is the one component [of the university] that affected people the most.

When asked what conditions constitute a library "emergency," bringing it to a high level of administrative concern, one CAO gave the following response:

> I would be very upset if anybody allowed [an emergency situation] to develop. I suppose that if for a period of time we had had no new acquisitions . . . so that the library, for all practical purposes, was no longer a functional entity, then it would have to have a high priority to bring it up [to functional levels]. But if that were allowed to happen, I would suspect that the academic units would have devolved into mediocrity as well . . . . A top-ranked university would not allow either to happen.

Another CAO suggested that the library becomes a top priority when rapid growth in enrollment requires additional library space.

Four of the universities participating in the study have recently built, have currently in construction, or have plans to build within the year a new science library. The fifth participant has specific plans to substantially increase library expenditures in medical and health-related fields over the next few years; it is the only institution in which the institution's emphasis on the development of new instructional and research programs includes the library. When asked why they were building a science library, the other administrators merely indicated that the current facility is no longer sufficient to meet students' needs. No direct relationship was made between a priority formally established by the university to improve or increase program development in the sciences and the library.

To summarize the responses to question 3, CEOs and CAOs were generally reluctant to distinguish between institutional priorities and mission or to establish priorities among the teaching, research, and service components of the mission. None of the administrators established a direct connection between any institutional priority to improve programs and the library. They identified access to library resources as important to graduate and research needs, in general, and study hall space important to undergraduate instruction, in general.

Question 4: Some research suggests that university administrators view what faculty and students say about the library as more important than

comparison to other libraries. How do you feel about this observation?
The final interview question instigated a discussion of specific ways in
which the centrality of the library is indicated. Subquestions helped determine which university constituents or units are more likely to influence administrative decisions regarding the library. Subquestions also
cited indicators of academic *unit* centrality that may apply to academic
library centrality.[3] A laundry list (figure 8 in chapter 3) of possible indicators of academic library centrality, drawn from the literature, served as
prompts for very specific responses from the interviewees. If the interviewee had not addressed the indicator in previous comments, he was
prompted during this phase of the interview. The discussion below is a
synthesis of responses to the specific indicators on the list. Most responses
to this laundry list were brief.

Previous research suggests that faculty and student comments about
the library are more important to administrators than comparisons to
other libraries. All but two of the interviewees agreed. For example, one
administrator in the pilot study suggested that "numbers alone do not
tell you if the collection is suitable for academic programs, for students
or faculty." Another specific comment was:

> I'm not interested in comparisons. I'm interested that students
> have access to everything they need in the appropriate time
> periods they need it . . . . The development of faculty is also
> important, especially for a young faculty member [who is at
> the beginning of his or her academic career]. I may pay atten-
> tion to faculty on a general scale, but if you want immediate
> action, send me young faculty or students.

One CAO commented that both local opinion and national reputation are important. Whatever the reputation of a nearby research library, he said, "If we have a problem on this campus, then that's a problem." Several interviewees questioned collection size as a basis for comparisons, with one suggesting that the level of technological innovation
is also a legitimate basis for comparisons with other institutions.

National reputation and ARL ranking were generally discounted by
most interviewees, particularly those from institutions with low ARL
ranking and no ARL membership. For instance, one response was that

quality at the local level is more important than national comparisons. Another response follows:

> The prestige of the library is related to the prestige of the university. You can't separate it. You don't have a library with a prestigious reputation without a university with a prestigious reputation.

The CEO from the university that does not currently hold ARL membership responded that ARL is not a significant indicator of library centrality. He also said, "If I had the best health sciences library on the East Coast, that's something I'd talk about." At least one other administrator emphatically denied that ARL ranking is an indication of library centrality. An administrator at an institution without ARL ranking disagreed. He stated that ARL membership is an indication of library quality and that his university will move toward that ideal.

From an obviously different perspective, both administrators at the university with the highest ARL ranking and with the longest history of library collection-building responded quite adamantly that national reputation and prestige are extremely important indicators of the library's centrality. As indicated in the preceding discussion, their university community gives great weight to the symbolic role of this library. Both men indicated that "in many ways [comparative] measures are more important than direct feedback that you get from faculty or students." This feedback, they feel, comes from a small, dissatisfied segment of the university community. Both men qualified their assertion by adding that comparative measures must be based on similar institutions. On the other hand, the CEO also said, "I'm much more interested in how well what we have serves the needs of the campus than I am in comparing it with some other library."

When asked to name the individuals, departments, or units on campus whose arguments are most cogent regarding library decisions, most interviewees cited formal mechanisms for organizational communication: library committees, administrative councils, student organizations, library directors, academic deans, faculty senates, and community support groups. Several interviewees dealt directly with library matters only when there was a specific problem that someone wanted to resolve (e.g., extending library hours on weekends or evenings; inability to locate a specific monograph on campus; the need for additional journal subscriptions). The location of the new sciences library and the percentage of the university's total budget allocated for library programs are examples of concerns brought to administrators by faculty or students.

When pressed to be more precise in identifying informal influences, most interviewees cited nothing more specific than "faculty" or "students." Despite the established view that universities function as political systems, none of the interviewees was willing to discuss political or differing levels of influence within the university. One CEO went so far as to identify "mathematicians" (regarding a departmental library) and "library-intense disciplines" such as history as more vocal in expressing their concerns about the library. Even these examples, however, were called "vocal" rather than influential. Both administrators at one university found that arguments delivered on behalf of the library are more convincing when they do not come from the library director or librarians. One interviewee remarked that "librarians do a poor job of selling to the members of the community—faculty, administration, students— the importance of the library." Interestingly, both faculty and students at this university made organized appeals for additional library services and extended hours.

Three items included on the laundry list of possible indicators derive from the literature on academic departmental centrality: innovation or creativity of librarians; instructional or research collaborations between librarians and other faculty members; and involvement of librarians in the faculty senate or university committee structure. Most of the interviewees saw these activities as desirable, but of little importance as indications of a library's centrality. Two interviewees suggested that national recognition of librarians or their programs is more important to them than librarians' research or involvement in university decisions. However, the following statement sums up the majority viewpoint: "These things are consistent with, and supportive of, centrality but not real measures [of centrality]."

Campus visibility, as an indicator of library centrality, received mixed responses. In many cases, the discussion of campus visibility led to discussion of the symbolic role of the library (described previously in this chapter). Several interviewees talked about the physical presence of the library building and a sense of place. When prompted to consider campus visibility in terms of librarians' interactions with others, most administrators were noncommittal. The following response was typical:

> I don't know. The library can be central; the librarian doesn't have to be. The university librarian is a very prominent member of the academic community. Some [librarians] are more prominent than others, but I'm not sure that that means the library is more central.

Often linked to comments on campus visibility were comments on the acquisition of outside funding as an indicator of centrality. Several interviewees found outside funding irrelevant for the academic library, particularly because libraries are not research-generating units; outside funding is less available for libraries than for other academic units. Instead, "the library should be the recipient of a proportion of all funds brought in" by other units. Although the administrators viewed research funding as extremely important to the university, they considered several academic units, including the library, to be "just as central to the educational process" as any unit that draws outside funding. On the other hand, some of the participating institutions are involved in development programs that include the library. One interviewee, for example, stated that the visibility of the campus library translates into enormous gifts. Because students who have gone through this university have developed respect for the strength and scale of this library, it is very effective in raising money from alums.

Responses about the quality of library resources, services, and personnel were generally very brief. Only one interviewee stated that he does not view quality as an indicator of centrality. Instead, he expects *each* unit to be of high quality. Another comment was:

> What we need [in a university library] is quality service . . . that's what makes the library a central resource.

Comments on the use of library services and resources were similarly brief; however, there was less agreement among interviewees. Some administrators suggested that "an unused library would not be very central" and "if [the library is] not used, it's not as needed." One CAO believed that use is currently an important indicator of library centrality. He also observed that changes in technology raise questions that are influencing his view.

Comments on geographic uniqueness and relationships with other libraries as indicators of academic library centrality were often related. The universities in the study were chosen, in part, because of their geographic location: Some were included specifically because they are isolated from other research libraries; others were included because of their proximity to other research libraries. Some administrators suggested that geographic uniqueness relates more to the university than to the library. Those in isolated areas found geographic uniqueness to be important to the library's centrality, as shown in this comment:

> [Geographic uniqueness is an indicator of library centrality] certainly at this institution. We're the only research library around for miles. Our library is central in many ways, not only in the center of campus, in the dead center of the state, in Centre County.

As expected, administrators from urban environments were less concerned with geographic uniqueness and emphasized the use of information technology to connect resources. One CAO stated that regardless of geography, there is a need for more collaborative collection development among university libraries.

To sum up, the predominant responses of CEOs and CAOs to question 4 were nonspecific. They named faculty, students, and formal vehicles of communication (e.g., councils, committees) as the voices most influential in decisions regarding library services and resources. In unusual circumstances, an individual administrator said that an indicator of *departmental* centrality also applied to the library. But, in general, administrators viewed none of these indicators as particularly indicative of *library* centrality.

Wrap-up Questions
As is customary, the interviews concluded with a series of wrap-up ques-

tions. Answers to two of these questions were surprisingly relevant to the central purpose of the interviews and, as a result, are discussed below. Usually, administrators from the same institution gave similar responses. The questions were:

1. What makes you most proud of this library? What makes you least proud?

2. Are there ways in which the library or library staff have helped you in your job lately (exclusive of library projects)?

The most frequent response to the first question was quality or attitude of the library faculty and staff. Among the interviewees, there was a distinct recognition of the service attitude of the library's staff. According to one CEO, "there is a real, 'service-to-the-university' attitude." Another administrator commented that "even in the toughest of times, our library staff goes the extra mile to find what you need, even if it is not on the shelf." One administrator said that he is most pleased when a student comes to his office and tells him about successfully getting research information with help from the library staff. Others commented on the sophistication of the staff, observing that the library faculty and staff are "strong and active nationally."

In contrast to comments made during the body of the interviews, the size and quality of the collection or the library's national reputation and ARL ranking made administrators proud. For example, one CEO stated that his greatest pride was in the "consistently high ranking [of the library] in credible polls." Both administrators from the university with the highest ARL ranking cited the library's collection as their greatest source of pride. One of these men emphasized his admiration of the vision of "founding fathers" who consciously set out to build a strong library from the beginning of the university. Regarding the institution's high ARL ranking, he added:

That history is both a challenge and an inspiration.

Several interviewees commented on their pride in the new science libraries on their campuses. Another administrator was proud of the community's support of the campus library.

Comments about the library services or resources that make the administrators least proud focused on space shortage and poor facilities, with blame placed not on the library administrator but on university finances. Other interviewees were unhappy that library collections are small and underdeveloped; others were not satisfied with the level of technology currently in place in the campus libraries. Interviewees were least proud of certain library services, observing that "It's a very good collection of books, but I'm not sure it's that good a library in terms of services." Finally, one CEO cited the "bureaucracy" of the library as the most frustrating issue; he offered the example of "questions about things like faculty status versus getting the job done."

Only two of the twelve individuals interviewed gave positive responses to the question, How has the library or library staff helped you?. In both cases, the library or library staff had provided articles, university archival materials, or reference assistance. No other administrators gave examples of ways in which the library or library staff had helped them directly in their work, except in providing information about the library and its operations. For example, one administrator responded:

> They are helping me understand and be more sensitive to the complexities of [library management] and how we best function in a time which is at best strapped for financial resources and in times that are transitional in function and vision.

Summary
In general, responses to question 1 (What does the phrase, "The library is the heart of the university" mean, if anything, to you?) were rhetorical descriptions of the academic library's place as a repository and symbol of the accumulation of knowledge and culture. Three administrators did not agree with the metaphor; instead, they viewed faculty or students as "the heart of the university." Most interviewees were not comfortable equating the metaphor with the university library mission. They suggested that the "heart of the university" metaphor is an exaggeration that does not address the practical reasons for library collections and services. In general, the library was perceived as having a strong symbolic role, in both intellectual and physical senses.

Responses to question 2 (Some institutions define centrality in terms of contributions to their mission and some in terms of connections between academic units. Which would you use?) indicated that the interviewees generally applied both definitions of centrality to the academic library. The administrators showed a slight preference for the definition that emphasized the library's contributions to the university mission. The most critical library resources or services cited by the interviewees were access to resources in the library's collection or in other libraries' collections or databases. The work of librarians in obtaining those resources was also considered a critical service. In response to question 3, interviewees were reluctant to specify priorities among the traditionally accepted components of a university mission. When pressed, however, most cited the conventional order—teaching, research, service. The participants identified contributions of the library to the teaching and research components of the mission, especially the importance of library collections to graduate research programs, but most comments were quite general.

Most interviewees agreed with statements found in the literature that administrators place a higher value on what faculty and students have to say about the library than on comparisons to other libraries (question 4). Both administrators from the institution with the highest ARL ranking were exceptions who felt that national reputation is a strong indicator of library centrality. Interviewees did not identify a specific group on campus as more persuasive in arguing for library funding. Faculty and students, in general, are influential. Several areas reported in the literature as indicative of academic unit centrality were described as "consistent with, and supportive of, centrality but not measures of centrality": innovation/creativity of librarians; instructional or research collaborations between librarians and other faculty; and librarians' involvement in the faculty senate or other university committee structure. Administrators made positive comments about campus visibility, the acquisition of outside funding, use, and quality as indicators of academic library centrality. None, however, said these were essential in making the library central. Finally, the wrap-up questions elicited specific examples, sometimes contradicting previous comments, of what the interviewees value most about library services and resources. These examples included quality and attitude of the library staff, size and quality of the library's collections, and national recognition or ranking of the library.

The interview responses summarized in this chapter give empirical evidence of what university administrators value about their libraries and librarians. The next chapter considers what these findings say about the library's centrality and what it means in theory and practice.

Notes

1. Larry L. Hardesty and David Kaser, "What Do Academic Administrators Think about the Library?" A Summary Report to the Council on Library Resources. (Grant CLR 8018-A, Feb. 1990, photocopy), introduction.

2. Ibid.

3. These questions were suggested by research on subunit power within universities. For more detail, see Deborah Jeanne Grimes, "Centrality and the Academic Library" (Ph.D. diss., University of Alabama, 1993).

5. User Success through Service, Access, and Tradition

In the preceding chapters, clues about indicators of academic library centrality were sought in the literature of organization theory and in the comments of university administrators. Before defining academic library centrality in this chapter, it is necessary first to discuss what academic library centrality is *not*. Those indicators about academic libraries that have little meaning to administrators will be eliminated from the list of possibilities. Because some long-held beliefs and much-argued issues, such as faculty status, are based on indicators this study shows *not* to be related to the library's centrality, it is necessary to take a closer look at the implications of these findings for practice. Because the study showed that some other indicators of the library's centrality are valued by university administrators, these must be examined carefully for their relevance to both theory and practice in librarianship. Finally, when all is said and done, the metaphor of the library as the heart of the university must be abandoned and other metaphors that contribute to a more realistic understanding of the academic library and its campus relationships must be considered. The concluding section of this chapter proposes one such metaphor.

What Academic Library Centrality Is Not

The interviews with leading academic administrators show that neither of the definitions of centrality neatly delineates academic library centrality. One definition proposed by Judith Dozier Hackman emphasizes an academic department's contribution to, or congruence with, the university's mission and can be called the "mission congruence" definition of centrality. The other, proposed by Hanna Ashar, stresses interconnectedness, or connections between academic departments, as a source of influence within the university.[1] The interviewees in this study were reluctant to choose one or the other; in fact, they specifically applied *both* definitions to the academic library. When pressed, the administrators in the study indicated a slight preference for the mission congruence definition of subunit centrality. Hackman's definition of *core* units as those that are essential to the university is clearly applicable to the academic library, and university administrators often used the same language in describing the mission of the academic library or its symbolic role on campus. At the same time, interviewees agreed that Ashar's connectivity definition of centrality is applicable to the academic library. Yet they invariably discounted the *measures* of connectivity identified by Ashar and others, such as the number of instructional and research collaborations and the amount of faculty involvement in the faculty senate and university committee structure. Thus, academic library centrality is *not* defined simply as mission congruence or as interconnectedness; instead, it reflects both components and requires different measures or indicators than some of those found to be appropriate for the academic *department*.

How do we identify, then, indicators of academic *library* centrality that fit both definitions? The grounded theory approach to generating concepts from data enables us to link academic library centrality with what university administrators have said. The term *empirical indicator (EI)* is used as an action or relationship that illustrates the concept under study. Although in experimental research the term *empirical* means specifically observed behavior or measurable activity, in grounded research, it refers to comments made by the interviewees. A list of possible indicators of academic library centrality (see figure 8 in chapter 3) was drawn from studies on resource allocation and retrenchment in higher education and other research. Results of this study showed that, indeed, administrators considered some items on the list to be indicative of academic library centrality. They viewed others, called "nonindicators" in the following discussion, differently. Nonindicators are identified below in figure 9.

In other words, university administrators gave little merit to innovation or creativity by librarians on their campuses. Unless librarians' originality related to information technology, such as the development of local area networks or electronic connections to other research libraries, administrators did not view creativity or innovation as significant indicators of the library's centrality to the university.[2] Similarly, instructional or research collaborations between librarians and other faculty were not recognized by administrators as reflections of the library's centrality. Most of the interviewees made perfunctory comments in response to specific questions about research and instruction conducted by librarians. The interviewees saw no connection between library centrality and a librarian's involvement in either the committee structure of the university or its faculty senate. It was not important to administrators for librarians to participate in the collegial decision-making process. Furthermore, it was not important to most administrators for librarians to have any visibility as individuals on campus. The interviewees gave little value to the activities of librarians outside the library. The only campus visibility valued was the symbolic presence of the library, which was quite

---

Figure 9. Indicators of Academic Unit/Departmental Centrality Not Found to Be Indicative of Academic Library Centrality

What Academic Library Centrality Is *Not*

> Innovation or creativity of librarians (except as applied to information technology)
>
> Instructional or research collaborations between librarians and other faculty
>
> Librarians' involvement in the faculty senate or university committee structure
>
> Acquisition of outside funding (unless related to a long history of library excellence)
>
> Campus visibility (except as related to the symbolic presence of the campus library; not related to the visibility of librarians on campus)

important to some administrators. Finally, attracting donations and winning research grants were not expected of librarians by university administrators. Most of the interviewees noted that such funding is difficult for librarians and library directors to gain on their own and that "the library should be a recipient of a proportion of all funds brought in" by other units.

The identification of these nonindicators of library centrality is important because they have not previously been identified and because they are often cited in relation to tenure and status requirements for academic librarians. As librarians wrestle with the issue of faculty status, they often attempt to wear some of the same badges of status applied to teaching faculty: research and publication, instructional collaboration, involvement in the faculty senate or university committee structure, visibility on campus, and acquisition of research grants and outside funding. The university administrators who participated in this study, however, attached no importance to librarians' activities in any of these areas.

Similar observations have been made by Steve Marquardt, who participated in a survey of fifteen editors and readers at ACRL:

> Some research universities give disproportionate weight to librarians' publications over their service in educating and training faculty and students in the changing world of information access and management. As a dean or provost, I would be concerned about the service output of the library, how it was leveraging the learning of our students, the research of our faculty, and the productivity and information literacy for our graduates.[3]

It may be argued that the number of participants in the study is small, but it must also be noted that the administrators in the study are influential career academics who served in faculty or administrative positions at, collectively, thirty-eight institutions. Although this is but one perspective among campus constituents served by the library, and although administrators may in fact use the library the least, they are the most direct and powerful influences on campus funding patterns, space and building allocations, ultimate choices and decisions regarding curricula and programs,[4] and general technology investments for the university. None of the other constituents affects these important influences on the capabilities of the library more strongly. Seen in this light, faculty status measured by teaching departmental criteria is a mantle that does not fit academic librarians and does not provide them with any power: The emperor is wearing no clothes. A struggle for faculty status based on teaching faculty criteria depends, therefore, on nonindicators of library centrality and probably is a waste of valuable time and effort.

At the same time, organizational status per se is important to more than personal ego. Status obviously affects salary level, which in turn affects recruitment to the profession and retention of good librarians and library administrators. The effects of status on individual position within the university—i.e., peer groups and participation in management decisions and institutional planning—affect the opportunities of librarians to gather the resources and information necessary to meet the information and research needs of library users. Learning how to influence student learning and facilitate research requires involvement with the academic community, but in a different way than general committee work or research collaboration. Librarians should seek a different type of academic status that will be more highly regarded by top administrators and will provide a better fit for academic librarians than faculty status. Librarians *are* different from teaching faculty—in academic preparation, in working situations, in their day-to-day activities, in their relationships with students and faculty, and in the instructional environment in which they work (which is often a one-on-one or tool-specific encounter). In fact, these differences enable librarians to fill a distinctive niche within the university that can support the goals of other campus constituents well. The present study shows that this niche is where librarians are most valued by university administrators. This does not mean that librarians are not educators but, rather, that the fit between what librarians do and what is more valued by campus decision makers may be better realized through the identification and promotion of value-added services provided by librarians to the academic community. In the words of Carla J. Stoffle, Robert Renaud, and Jerilyn R. Veldof: "librarians must be sure that their work, activities, and tasks add value to the customer . . . ."[5] By concentrating on an institutional status based

on value-added information services, academic librarians come much
closer to fulfilling their mission and achieving centrality within the university.

Academic Library Centrality: What It Is

Although identification of nonindicators gives an idea of what is *not*
important to academic administrators, the identification of actual indicators offers much to both theory and practice. Several indicators of
academic library centrality can be derived from the interview results.
Presented in figure 10, these indicators generally show, with no particular rank, a wide range of library resources, services, or facilities identified
by university decision makers as meaningful to library centrality (descriptions are included in appendix A). As expected, some indicators
detected in previous studies on academic *departmental* centrality were
found to be appropriate to the academic library: geographic uniqueness;
quality and expertise of personnel; community or external financial support (including alumni support); current reputation or prestige; a history of reputation or excellence (including, in this case, ARL ranking);
uniqueness of services (i.e., criticality or substitutability of the unit);
and the number of people affected, including the number of graduate
students (viewed as level of use in the case of the academic library).
These are indicators one through seven in figure 10. Also as expected,
some indicators identified in the present study were unique to academic
libraries: symbolic role; storage and retrieval of information; service attitude or responsiveness of library personnel; faculty and student opinions; general quality or reputation of the university; providing good information to CEOs and CAOs about the library; speed of responses and
acquisition of information; access to information or mechanisms for
access (including current levels of technology); convenience to users;
size and quality of the library's collection (including periodicals); specific services offered by the library; practical role and use of the library;
quality of facilities provided by the library (including the provision of
study space and a warm environment); and university priorities (related
to research priorities, development and growth of disciplines, and specific inclusion of the library in strategies to improve programs). These
indicators, numbered eight through twenty-one in figure 10, are unique
to libraries in the sense that they have not previously been identified in

Figure 10. General Indicators of Academic Library Centrality

EI1:	Geographic uniqueness
EI2:	Quality and expertise of personnel
EI3:	Community or external financial support, including alumni support
EI4:	Current reputation or prestige of the library
EI5:	History of reputation or excellence of the library, including ARL ranking
EI6:	Uniqueness of services offered (i.e., criticality and substitutability)
EI7:	Number of people affected, including number of graduate students (i.e., use)
EI8:	Symbolic role
EI9:	Information storage and retrieval
EI10:	Service attitude/responsiveness of library personnel
EI11:	Faculty and student opinion
EI12:	Quality or reputation of the university
EI13:	Providing good information about the library to the CEOs/CAOs
EI14:	Speed of responses and acquisition of information
EI15:	Access to information and mechanisms for access, including current level of technology
EI16:	Convenience to users
EI17:	Size and quality of the library's collection, including periodicals
EI18:	Specific services offered by the library
EI19:	Practical role and use of the library
EI20:	Quality of facilities provided by the library, including the provision of study space and a warm environment
EI21:	University priorities (i.e., research priorities are linked to library collections and services); development and growth of disciplines; specific inclusion of library in plans to improve programs

ACADEMIC LIBRARY CENTRALITY

relation to academic departmental centrality. In some cases, these indicators are activities not conducted by academic departments (e.g., retrieval of information, providing mechanisms for access to information).[6]

These findings show that certain services, resources, or facilities provided by the academic library are relevant indicators of academic library centrality in relation to the general mission of the university of teaching, research, and service. Further consideration of the indicators suggests that some are more closely associated with one of the three components of the university mission than with another. Because the interviewees made virtually no comments about library contributions to service, only teaching and research are addressed. Although there is some overlap (see EI1 through EI11), figures 11 and 12 differentiate between indicators of academic library centrality.[7] Consequently, one interpretation of the interview results is to group indicators of academic library centrality according to components of the university mission. Certain indicators of academic library centrality are more pertinent to research, whereas others are more pertinent to teaching, as identified in figures 11 and 12, respectively.

Building a Framework for Academic Library Centrality

Viewing indicators of academic library centrality according to the teaching and research components of the university mission is useful in practice. Such a view helps libraries focus on how best to serve graduates and undergraduates; however, it offers very little information for building a theory. Consequently, the data gathered in this study must be distilled in some other way to find a more relevant framework for further study. Constance Ann Mellon's guidelines for intensive analysis in naturalistic inquiry and the logico-deductive pattern of Jacqueline Fawcett and Florence S. Downs suggested that key categories will emerge from grouping the indicators in different ways, as illustrated in the linkage model in figure 13.[8]

Two broad categories of empirical indicators are immediately evident in the examination of research data: service and access. In fact, both categories were explicitly mentioned by virtually every interviewee in both the pilot and formal studies, and both are unique to academic library centrality (in the sense of applicability to specific library activities). The original list of indicators may be regrouped as shown in figure

Figure 11. *Indicators of Academic Library Centrality Related to the Research Component of the University Mission*

EI1:	Size and quality of the library's collection, including periodicals
EI2:	Specific services offered by the library
EI3:	Practical role and use of the library
EI4:	Faculty and student opinion
EI5:	Quality and expertise of personnel
EI6:	Quality and reputation of the university
EI7:	Information storage and retrieval
EI8:	University priorities (especially the development and growth of research disciplines); specific inclusion of the library in plans to improve programs
EI9:	Providing good information about the library to the CEOs/CAOs
EI10:	Speed of responses and acquisition of information
EI11:	Access to information and mechanisms for access, including periodicals
EI12:	Geographic uniqueness
EI13:	Uniqueness of services offered (i.e., criticality and substitutability)
EI14:	Community or external financial support, including alumni support
EI15:	Current reputation or prestige of the library
EI16:	History of reputation or excellence of the library, including ARL ranking
EI17:	Number of people affected, especially graduate students (i.e., use)
EI18:	Symbolic role

Left margin label: ACADEMIC LIBRARY CENTRALITY RELATED TO THE RESEARCH COMPONENT OF THE UNIVERSITY MISSION

Figure 12. *Indicators of Academic Library Centrality Related to the Teaching Component of the University Mission*

ACADEMIC LIBRARY CENTRALITY RELATED TO THE TEACHING COMPONENT OF THE UNIVERSITY MISSION	
EI1:	Size and quality of the library's collection, including periodicals
EI2:	Specific services offered by the library
EI3:	Practical role and use of the library
EI4:	Faculty and (especially) student opinion
EI5:	Quality and expertise of personnel
EI6:	Quality and reputation of the university
EI7:	Information storage and retrieval
EI8:	University priorities (especially the development and growth of disciplines); specific inclusion of the library in plans to improve programs
EI9:	Providing good information about the library to the CEOs/CAOs
EI10:	Speed of responses and acquisition of information
EI11:	Access to information and mechanisms for access, including current level of technology
EI12:	Quality of library facilities (especially including the provision of study space and a warm environment)
EI13:	Service attitude or responsiveness of library personnel
EI14:	Convenience to users

14. It is also easy to see that many indicators listed under Service are related to teaching, whereas many of those listed under Access are related to research.

We already know several effective means through which many, if not all, of these indicators of service and access can be measured or evaluated. For example, many of the service indicators—attitude and responsiveness of librarians, expertise of librarians (as expressed in the *opinions* of users based on their experiences with librarians at a particular library), quality of facilities, convenience—are traditionally evaluated through

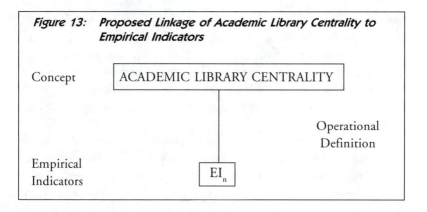

Figure 13: **Proposed Linkage of Academic Library Centrality to Empirical Indicators**

Concept

ACADEMIC LIBRARY CENTRALITY

Operational
Definition

Empirical
Indicators

EI_n

Figure 14: **Indicators of Academic Library Centrality Grouped by Broad Categories of Service and Access**

SERVICE

Quality and expertise of personnel
Number of people affected (i.e., use)
Service attitude/responsiveness of librarians
Faculty and student opinion
Providing good information about the library to the CEOs/CAOs
Convenience to users
Specific services offered by the library
Quality of facilities provided by the library, including the
    provision of study space and warm environment

ACCESS

Geographic uniqueness
Uniqueness of services offered (i.e., criticality and substitutability)
Information storage and retrieval
Speed of responses and acquisition of information
Access to information and mechanisms for access, including
    current level of technology
Size and quality of the library's collection, including periodicals
University priorities; development and growth of disciplines;
    specific inclusion of library in strategies to improve programs

the use of user opinion or satisfaction surveys, focus groups, or suggestion boxes. Specific services offered by the library, such as reference services, are easily measured. For example, Peter Hernon and Charles R. McClure suggested measuring referrals to other libraries, analysis of staffing patterns, and review of staff training and professional development in order to assess the library's "capacity to provide reference services."[9] The quality of librarians can be assessed through regular performance review (regardless of tenure or continuing service status) and review of credentials and professional development activities. More controversial, but more valuable, are obtrusive and unobtrusive means of testing reference librarians. F. Wilfred Lancaster described, for example, simulation studies in which reference librarians were given sets of questions to be answered while under observation by an evaluator, and volunteers or "surrogate users" were employed to pose reference questions and record the details of the librarian's response (e.g., attitude, length of time, thoroughness).[10]

There are several established means through which the number of people affected by the library can be measured. Facilities use rate or building use rate can be quantitatively measured by headcounts at hourly intervals (general or in specific service areas) and by door counters. Such information can be an effective means of identifying how and when library facilities and resources succeed or fail to meet the needs of library users at a given time for a given institution. Results of such studies can lead to changes in staffing patterns, "express" public-access terminals or circulation stations, and other focused improvements in service. For example, Nancy A. Van House, Beth T. Weil, and Charles R. McClure recommended the use of these methods to answer the question: What is the probability that a user will find a seat, a piece of equipment, or a public services staff member available?[11]

Two related indicators, the number of users and the practical role of the library, can be assessed through a simple review of collection and circulation statistics. Although none of the methods of user analysis currently in use are cast in terms of centrality, they can be focused more specifically to do so. For example, useful information emphasizing *centrality* to specific user needs can be gained by examining circulation, use, and nonuse statistics in specific contexts (e.g., graduate versus undergraduate use, use by specific university departments, use according to time of day, etc.). Paul

Metz proposed several means of user analysis in *The Landscape of Literatures: Use of Subject Collections in a University Library*.[12]

User opinion and satisfaction surveys may also be applied to the access indicators of academic library centrality. Measurement of information storage and retrieval, speed of responses (for specific questions as well as for retrieval of off-campus documents), access to information, and mechanisms for access to information, for example, can be addressed with evaluation techniques for literature searching for relevance, precision, recall, novelty, and response time. Library collections of all types can be measured by absolute size, size in relation to variables such as subject areas, number and type of unfilled requests, and formulas (such as the ACRL and Clapp-Jordan formulas). Expert opinion or expert judgment can be used to assess collection quality, as can comparison to standard or recommended bibliographies and analysis of actual use.[13]

Geographic uniqueness is measured by the university's distance to another research facility or library. The related indicators of uniqueness of services, criticality, and substitutability can be based on a comparison of a library's services and resources with those available from other campus units (such as departmental resources, the bookstore, or the campus computer center). An assessment of the criticality of the library's resources may be made through analysis of unfilled requests to determine which resources have been specifically requested that were *not* available to meet a specific user need—and why not. Perhaps more significantly, analyses of user and nonuser needs shed light on the criticality and substitutability of academic library resources and services. Lancaster pointed out:

> If evaluation activities focus only on the demands (i.e., expressed needs) of present users and fail to study the needs lying behind these demands, or if they ignore the latent needs of present nonusers, the danger exists of creating a self-reinforcing situation.[14]

Budget allocations and planning documents can be examined to verify the degree to which the campus library is a priority concern of the university. Further evidence of academic library centrality can be seen in plans to develop or enhance programs or disciplines that specifically outline the strengths and weaknesses of the library resources, facilities, or services needed for support.

With these measurement and evaluative techniques in mind, the following working definition of *academic library service* may be applied: Academic library service consists of all those elements that render the library usable, including the attitude and responsiveness of its librarians as well as the state of its facilities and the range of functions and resources available to users. Similarly, the following working definition of *access* may be applied: Academic library access consists of collections of information and research materials made available by the library to the user (regardless of the location of the user or of the materials) as well as mechanisms provided by the library that enable the user to retrieve those materials (regardless of format or location). In this sense, the source of the materials is irrelevant; it is the delivery of the information or document, whether owned or not, and how the information or document is located that constitute access. Consequently, these working definitions of service and access encompass both the actual academic library and what Carol A. Hughes calls the "'logical library,' which is a range of services and collections made accessible through networks."[15]

The remaining indicators of academic library centrality can be viewed as the result, in some way, of tradition. For example, financial contributions to the library from the community and alumni were identified by interviewees as indicators of academic library centrality. In one case, it was the *tradition* of alumni or external financial support, rather than isolated donations, that was important to university administrators. As suggested above, faculty and student opinion are ways to measure library services and indicate an academic library's centrality. By extension, a *history* or tradition of user satisfaction can be cited as an indicator of academic library centrality. This type of history is evidence that the library is regularly and consistently responsive to user needs.

The size and quality of the library's collection, identified as an indicator of centrality, is also related to a tradition of both financial support and professional expertise. In addition, the reputation of an academic library, identified as an indicator, is generally based on its history of budgetary support, collection development, and staff size. Membership in ARL, for example, is not awarded until an institution has maintained an acceptable index score (based on several quantitative measures) for at least four years. Most institutions build to the acceptable level over a considerable length of time. As handed down, year after year, the support required to create outstanding library collections or to be accepted as an "ARL library" becomes a part of the university's library tradition. Similarly, the quality or reputation of a university is built over time; it is reflected in outside opinion, enrollment, prestigious research awards, and related events—as well as in the quality of its library.

As a result, the broad category of tradition can include measurable indicators of centrality such as the library's longevity, its budget history (the level of funding over the years), its history of financial support by the community or alumni, the quality and size of its collection, and its ARL ranking.

Although difficult to measure or quantify, the symbolic role of the library was quite important to the university administrators who participated in the study. The symbolism of the library as a reflection of the university's commitment to research and scholarship was potent at institutions with long histories and solid reputations as research institutions. In these cases, the library held both a physical presence and collection size and quality to match the institution's self-image. Interviewees related the symbolic role of the library to a tradition of faculty and student opinion that created strong alumni support of the institution. A regrouping of indicators drawn from figure 10 under the broad category of tradition is given in figure 15.

The working definition of *tradition* as a broad category of indicators of academic library centrality, then, is as follows: Academic library

---

Figure 15.   Indicators of Academic Library Centrality Grouped by the Broad Category of Tradition

Community or external financial support, including alumni support

Current reputation or prestige of the library

History of reputation or excellence of the library, including ARL membership

Symbolic role

Quality or reputation of the university

Size and quality of the library's collection

Faculty and student opinion (especially a history of satisfaction)

tradition is the accumulated experiences of the library, whether abstract (e.g., symbolic) or concrete (e.g., collection size), that shaped its present circumstances. This definition reflects the observation by Edward Shils that tradition is composed of "patterns inherited from the past as valid guides."[16] Subsequently, the broad categories of service, access, and tradition summarize and integrate the data from figure 10 and begin to complete the model of linkage between academic library centrality and empirical indicators (figure 16). From this model, three major categories of indicators of academic library centrality—service, access, and tradition— can be distilled from the range of possibilities .

The problems of manipulation, measurement, and ambiguity evident in the definitions of academic *unit* centrality (described in chapter 2) can be addressed through these three broad categories of indicators of academic library centrality. First, artificial manipulation of interdepartmental connections to increase unit power does not apply: The library already has genuine connections to all other academic units and usually has no student enrollment to share with other units. Second, a number of measures are regularly used in each of the broad categories of indicators of academic library centrality. Third, the categories of service, access, and tradition may be applied to the library of any institution of higher education, regardless of its mission or ambiguities in its mission. In fact, these categories are not bound by university priorities, which is troublesome in defining departmental centrality, or by type of academic institution. Indeed, they are useful at any level of academic library prac-

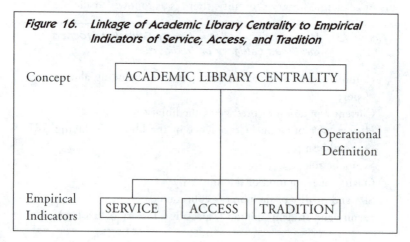

Figure 16.   Linkage of Academic Library Centrality to Empirical Indicators of Service, Access, and Tradition

Concept   ACADEMIC LIBRARY CENTRALITY

                                                    Operational
                                                    Definition

Empirical
Indicators   SERVICE   ACCESS   TRADITION

tice—college, university, or community college. As suggested by one interviewee, centrality is at issue regardless of the mission of the university.

Operational Definition of Academic Library Centrality

The ultimate goal of the study described in chapter 3 was to identify indicators of academic library centrality that link the concept with the practice of librarianship and show how centrality can be measured or determined. This leads to the question: *What theme explains or ties the data together?* In other words, is there a concept that embraces the categories of service, access, and tradition; links them to academic library centrality; and operationalizes the concept of centrality?

The obvious link is the user. This concept, however, is too broad. What we really need to know is what *about* the user links these three concepts in a way that informs our theory and practice. When the categories are considered further, it is possible to see that it is the *success* of the user that speaks to centrality; it is the *success* of the user (whether faculty, student, researcher, or administrator) that is affected by the service, access, and tradition of an academic library. An operational definition is the "empirical meaning" or statement of terms through which the concept can be measured or manipulated.[17] In this sense, user success is the operational definition linking academic library centrality with its indicators of service, access, and tradition. *User success* can be defined as the user's achievement of educational goals as a result of service, access, and tradition of the library associated with the user's academic institution. A user's short-term goal, for example, may be as simple as writing a critique of a poem. The library and librarians help the user succeed in this goal through services (such as hours of operation convenient to the user or direct reference assistance from a librarian), through its access (such as providing the text of the poem and literary criticism in one or more formats, print or electronic, and through bibliographic aids that help the user locate the criticism), and through tradition (the user is confident about locating what he or she needs because of past experience or the reputation of the librarians). A user's long-term goal may be to produce a dissertation that meets the requirements of the institution. The library's services (such as interlibrary loan), access (such as *Dissertation Abstracts Online*), and tradition (a history of collection development in the necessary subject fields) helps the user achieve this longer-term goal. User *success*, notably, is differentiated from user *satisfaction* (i.e., faculty and student opinion). User satisfaction is but one of several empirical indicators within the broad category of service. The definition of user success is illustrated schematically in figure 17: Library service combined with access and tradition yields a successful user.

Figure 17.   Schematic Illustration of User Success in the Academic Library

SERVICE + ACCESS + TRADITION ⎯⎯> USER SUCCESS

From this perspective, user success is a highly focused concept that requires a deep understanding of the information and service needs of students, researchers, and other significant library users. It encompasses standard academic library activities, resources, and services, but it requires a commitment to what Fred Heath has called "the agile organization."[18] To keep the library agile, academic librarians must confront the specter of obsolescence or failure to meet user needs and address specific weaknesses within the library. User success is also a broad concept that cuts across institutional boundaries; it is useful in all types of academic institutions with all types of users. User success is referenced in use studies, which are long-standing means of measuring certain aspects of library effectiveness, and it follows the contemporary emphasis on output measures of library effectiveness: "Output measures reflect user success in the library . . . , not simply library performance. The outcome is a function of the library, the user, and the library's success in anticipating the user's needs and assisting in the user's search."[19]

User success seems to provide a better focus for academic library performance than user satisfaction, which, when called customer satisfaction, is the pivotal concern of the total quality management (TQM) movement now in vogue in many academic institutions, including academic libraries. A focus on satisfaction alone seems to overlook the primary mission of the educational institution—which is to educate. The student is more than a customer in educational institutions; he or she is also the product of the institution. A customer, for example, merely purchases or buys a product or service. Education, by definition, is more than this: It is "the act or process of imparting or acquiring general knowledge and of developing the powers of reasoning and judgment."[20] The student does more than "buy" an educational service; the student receives something from the university (i.e., an education) and then *becomes* something more as a result (i.e., an individual with greater knowledge and better-developed powers of reasoning and judgment). Consequently, user success is a more complex concept than user satisfaction, appropriate to the more complex customer–product relationship of a university student to the institution.

Focusing on user success as an operational definition of academic library centrality requires academic librarians to identify various departmental priorities and hone academic library services and collections to meet specific needs. As such, user success meshes with the power/politics school of organization theory, which emphasizes the formation of coalitions between units to achieve goals. User success is a concept that reflects the greater emphasis placed by interviewees on the comments or opinions of faculty and staff (rather than on national rankings). The following statement by a CEO illustrates this point: "I'm much more interested in how well what we have serves the needs of the campus than I am in comparing it with some other library."

Additional examples may help to further clarify the concept. For instance, the success of the undergraduate student is conventionally viewed as dependent upon teaching (and the library's services that support that teaching) as well as the development of good study habits. This may account for the fact that study hall space was so frequently mentioned by university decision makers as an indicator of the library's centrality to the teaching component of the university mission. Study space becomes even more significant as a value-added service when the library's study spaces are "designed to provide technologies, information, and support services not available in other spaces used by students for study."[21]

In fact, there appears to be a resurgence in interest in the undergraduate library, or at least in providing specific services to undergraduates. This is evident in the "information commons" of the Leavey Library, the undergraduate library of the University of Southern California; the University of Iowa Information Arcade; and libraries in the

Maricopa County Community College District in Arizona. This approach to library service combines all information and information technology programs and services into one building and one network, allowing students to have information, resources, reference assistance, technical support, and tutorial services in one place. The Leavey Library embodies the concept of the "'teaching library,' a high-technology environment that offers skilled personnel and services to promote learning and teaching."[22] The teaching library is an example of focused and collaborative efforts to address service, access, and tradition that promote user success.

A focus on user success is directly related to the underlying assumption in the ACRL "Standards," which links the purpose of the academic library with "the level and *success* of scholarship and research."[23] The success of the graduate student or researcher, in contrast to the undergraduate, is generally related to his or her ability to produce research of sufficient quality acceptable to the scholarly community. This activity requires supportive materials made available through the university's library, whether through collection development, acquisitions on demand, or interlibrary loan. If these resources are not provided, the user does not achieve success through library service, access, or tradition, and thus must look elsewhere for the materials that will contribute to his or her success. As observed by Fred Heath, "By making themselves indispensable to scholars, librarians can prosper in the electronic age."[24]

This approach is not inconsistent with the professional concerns identified in chapter 1 (e.g., inadequate funding, lack of understanding of librarians' educational roles, lack of inclusion in campus information technologies decisions, lack of participation by librarians in the collegium, and so forth). Although results of this study show that nominal participation in the faculty senate and university committee structure is *not* indicative of academic library centrality, involvement in the collegium helps the academic librarian or CLO identify the specific library services or resources that are needed to contribute to the academic success of students or faculty. For example, the proactive stance advocated by Herbert S. White[25] is a means through which the academic librarian can reach into the university community and gain a better understanding of ways in which to help the academic library fulfill its mission. Similarly, involvement in decisions regarding campus information technologies will enable the academic librarian or CLO to help establish information policies and to build the information systems and networks, at both local and national levels, needed by students and faculty to succeed. The concept of user success, then, is a lens through which to focus on the ways in which the mission of the academic library can be fulfilled.

Two examples of output measures that can involve a focus on user success are the use of transaction log analyses and user success surveys. Today's online library systems automatically record transactions at public-access terminals, including the actual search terms entered by library users. When compiled into logs for specific time periods and analyzed, this information can be used to show exactly what search terms and strategies were used by students (to identify bibliographic instruction needs for users), peak time periods (to help determine staffing patterns), needed public-access screen changes (because of misleading information or poor online instructions), and other rich data that can be used to improve the services and means of access to information on campus.[26]

Finally, Van House, Weil, and McClure expanded the user satisfaction survey to provide library users with a means to rate their level of success in what they attempted to do on a particular visit to the campus library (e.g., looked for books, asked a reference question, studied, conducted a literature search, etc.).[27] On a specially designed form, library users are also asked how *easy* they found their particular task to be that day. Van House, Weil, and McClure further suggested that the results be analyzed by user subgroups to help identify differing service needs of library users. This is another tool librarians can use in academic libraries from the perspective of user success.

Based on the results of the study and subsequent analyses, it can be concluded that academic library centrality is operationally defined through user success. The completed pattern, as originally suggested in chapter 3, assumes the following shape (figure 18), where academic library centrality is operationally defined through user success and is linked to the practice of librarianship through empirical indicators in the broad categories of service, access, and tradition. *In simplest terms, academic library centrality is the promotion of user success.*

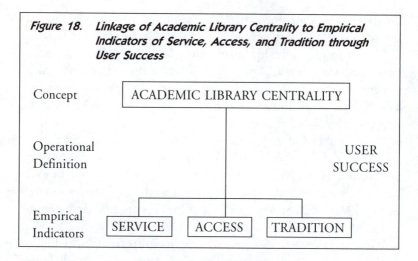

Figure 18.   Linkage of Academic Library Centrality to Empirical Indicators of Service, Access, and Tradition through User Success

From "The Heart of the University" to "Crossroads Community": A New Metaphor for the Academic Library

In chapter 1, it was found that the metaphor "the library is the heart of the university" holds little power for modeling or theory generation and gives little guidance for the practice of librarianship. In addition, the discussion in chapter 1 suggests that this metaphor has been used as an equivalent for the mission of the academic library. However, university administrators who participated in the study did not view the "heart of the university" metaphor as the equivalent of the academic library's mission. Instead, they viewed it to be an exaggeration of that mission.

Chapter 1 points to three major areas—instruction, funding, and the role of the library in campus decision-making and organizational structure—where academic libraries are stagnating or in decline. This stagnation and decline, at a time when the "heart of the university" metaphor has held sway, also point to the inadequacy of the metaphor. Although the CEOs and CAOs interviewed demonstrated that libraries on their campuses were better funded than on some other campuses, much of what they said also showed that the libraries fit the norms of decline. Thus, administrators saw teaching as one of the university's most important efforts, yet only one in seven of the universities studied had a specific plan for library contributions to teaching. Most of the interviewees spoke of study hall space as the most significant service provided by the library to undergraduates, were unsure of bibliographic instruction programs, and, even when directly questioned, cited no specific educational or instructional services provided by the library (other than general provision of books and periodicals). These administrators seemed to have little or no interest in librarians' participation in activities generally associated with teaching faculty or with institution-wide decision-making. In particular, the CLO and librarians in the participating universities were not significantly involved in determining university-wide information and telecommunications technology policies. Individual departments and academic units were acquiring database access directly, generally through grant monies and apparently without consideration of a central university information policy or plan. Most of the CEOs and CAOs interviewed said that they *expected* to see a major involvement in technology decisions by the CLO and librarians but did not suggest, in general, that their involvement was vital to campus technology decisions. One CEO admitted that he was playing a waiting game with the CLO, in which the success or failure of the CLO would be determined by the decisions made regarding technology and related expenditures of funds allocated for the library. Reflecting observations made in chapter 1, the CLOs and librarians in the universities studied here did not provide leadership in campus deliberations regarding information and communication technologies. If the "heart of the university" metaphor were truly effective, the library would not be isolated from campus instructional efforts nor would the CLO and librarians be shut out of decision-making, especially decision-making related to information and communication technologies. Thus, it is evident that the academic library community needs a more meaningful metaphor than "the library is the heart of the university."

Metaphors do more than "translate one realm into another;" they also suggest new ways to view and understand what is already known.[28] Consequently, an effective metaphor for the role of the academic library within the university should provide some new understanding or some new perspective from which to examine organizational relationships. One metaphor for the academic library, found in library literature and suggested by interviewees in the study described in previous chapters, is "the library is a gateway to information." University administrators used this metaphor to describe what they saw as the "new" role for academic libraries in the information age. But *gateway* is generally defined as an entrance or passageway, with "gate" implying a closed or controlled situation. The actions associated with a gate are to allow or restrict passage, bringing to mind the negative connotations of gatekeepers as barriers to communication. The current information environment, often characterized as an "explosion," is hardly closed or controlled. As an integral part of the current environment, the academic library is much more than a gateway.

Another popular metaphor, used in designing library services at some universities, is "the network is the library." Peter Lyman suggests that the network is a valid image of the library understood as a medium for the acquisition, storage, and circulation of texts, particularly if it leads to the creation of shared resources.[29] But this is a cold image of file servers and cables that, although encompassing much of the mechanics—or in this case, the electronics—of the virtual library, overlooks the human element involved in university life and focuses on the delivery system rather than the service components that are so important in academic librarianship.

An image that suits the situation better and provides an interesting perspective for viewing the relationship of the academic library to the university is that of "crossroads community." A *crossroads* is defined as "the point at which a vital decision is made" and "a main center of activity or assembly."[30] Initially, the image conjured up by "crossroads" may be that of small rural communities connected by county roads or older state highway systems. Such communities may consist only of gas stations and country stores (now sporting video rentals and tanning booths). Sometimes there are churches and sometimes, depending on the part of the country, there are old, now unused silos or cotton gins and railway stations. At the same time, this humble image is not the only one that can be conjured up with the words "crossroads community." The "community" part of the phrase implies connections, services, people, and resources. *Random House Webster's Electronic Dictionary* defines *community* as "a group of people who reside in a specific locality, share government, and often have a common cultural and historical heritage." The sense of community evident in crossroads community adds a warm, human element to the image, saying much about relationships among those who form the community.

Crossroads communities are not only rural in nature. What begins as a simple rural connecting point sometimes grows into a bustling center or township or even a large city. Ultimately, urbanization may connect a region of expanding crossroads communities into complex metropolitan centers. There are many crossroads communities, ranging in size and complexity along a continuum from the sleepy small town to the large metropolitan center. The people and resources that constitute a particular community have different needs that are filled through a crossroads connection; fulfilling needs is the important issue in a crossroads community, so small crossroads communities can be as viable to those who need them as large crossroads communities.

The crossroads community is a valuable way to consider the role of the academic library in the American university. The academic library is a scholarly community crossroads, affected by and affecting its environment, its technology, and its users. Just as a crossroads connects people to other places and other resources, the academic library connects students and faculty to other institutions and information sources. Like the crossroads community, the academic library offers the current technology for access—in this case, the information superhighway, an effective metaphor itself for global networking and with which the "crossroads" metaphor is consistent.

Crossroads communities that do not change with local needs die out because local users may, with improved transportation, more easily go to the commercial and urban centers that do fill their needs. We have all seen such communities that bear names from more prosperous times, often including "crossroads" in their titles. It is easy to understand why these once-promising sites are now merely ghost towns or tiny mercantile centers for the nearby rural community: The railroads that were once so important to the community are no longer used for travel or transport of goods; the cotton or corn crops that once needed silos and gins are now some other farm commodity; and, the national highway system has bypassed these once-important communities because of more effective leadership on the part of another community or because another site offered more resources to the highway planners and users.

The academic library can meet the same fate if it is not in tune with its users' needs and if it does not provide the most effective technology and resources available. This does not mean, however, that a specific technology determines the viability of the library or of the crossroads community. For example, abandoned railway stations in some crossroads communities are evidence that this mode of transportation (i.e., technology) was once popular and effective, offering safe, speedy transportation for both people and goods. Now, however, there are newer technologies that compete for personal and commercial transportation which make this mode obsolete for many communities. The community that focused on the technology, rather than the service, suffered. This is an important lesson offered through the "crossroads community" metaphor for the academic library: The library that loses sight of its mission by focusing instead on the mode of "transportation" or technology, if it survives at all, will not remain an important contributor to the community and its needs.

Does the metaphor "academic library as a crossroads community" meet the tests for sociological metaphors? Is it cogent? economical? isomorphic? Does it have range?[31] The concept of the academic library as a community certainly seems to be cogent and convincing. The library has an internal community of library resources and services (e.g., reference and information services, cataloging and technical services, user instruction, acquisitions) and an external community of teachers, researchers, and students, as well as campus telecommunications and computing resources and services. The common cultural and historical heritage aspect of community is also relevant to the academic library and the university, particularly given the important symbolic role held by the academic library in many universities.

The concept of the academic library as a crossroads is also appropriate, with its connections to campus resources, outside institutions, and larger networks. The *Random House Dictionary* definition of *crossroads* includes "a point at which a vital decision must be made" and "a main center of activity or assembly." It is one of the few places on campus that draws students and faculty from all departments to one physical location (i.e., a crossing of students and scholars from all disciplines). Both definitions are pertinent to the actual and symbolic connections made through the academic library by students and scholars. In fact, "crossroads" is sometimes applied to the academic library in the same way that "gateway" is used. The community aspect of the "crossroads community" metaphor, however, adds much more dimension and appeal to the image.

Is community crossroads an economical image? Unlike the word *heart* in the "heart of the university" metaphor, the metaphor's key word, *crossroads*, has only three definitions in the *Oxford English Dictionary*.[32] Two of these definitions are the literal application of the term: a road crossing another; the place where two roads cross each other (i.e., the intersection of roads). It is an economical term, then, that may have many visual images, but the implied relationships are always similar. Therefore, the "crossroads" metaphor meets the test of economy.

Finally, is the "crossroads" metaphor isomorphic, and does it provide a range of possible uses? That is, can a number of comparisons be made on a one-to-one basis within the implied relationships? The preceding discussion seems to do just that. The gas stations and country stores, with their select "new technologies," such as tanning beds and video rentals, are like small academic libraries that offer a few of the newer technologies—one or two stand-alone databases and limited connection to outside sources via dial access terminals. These libraries still offer the mainstays—books, periodicals, reference assistance—just as the country store offers bread, milk, and other traditional necessities. The abandoned cotton gin or silo of the community crossroads is reminiscent of the abandoned information storage technologies of eight-millimeter tapes, filmloops, and perhaps soon, microfilm and printed indexes found at academic library crossroads communities.

Like viable crossroads, both large and small, academic library crossroads that offer more than one mode of technology (i.e., transportation) and a larger array of community services prosper in meeting the needs of library users. Their offerings include such things as local area networks with access to several databases (CD-ROM or dial access), Internet and Web access, acquisitions on demand, and strong bibliographic instruction programs. The comparison can also be made, in terms of location, of the academic library on the university campus as an important physical presence that connects students and faculty with the resources and services they need to succeed in academe. This is the image of the "information commons" and "teaching library" proposed by Phillip Tompkins.[33] Furthermore, the library-as-crossroads image fits the library-without-walls or virtual library concept by emphasizing both services *and* connections between library users, wherever they are physically located, with electronic resources and services, wherever they are generated. The academic library remains the nexus through which such contacts are made, just as the crossroads connects the community to larger highway systems; but the community aspect of the "crossroads community" metaphor reflects how much more is offered by the academic library than a mere connecting point.

The study described in this book led to the identification of the concept of user success and its empirical indicators of academic library centrality. These, too, are consistent with the "community crossroads" metaphor. The thriving crossroads must have all these elements—access, service, and tradition. These include both basic and enhanced library services, such as the necessities provided by the country store or gas station, as well as sophisticated cultural agencies or social services provided in urban centers to promote research, service, and instruction. Library services are an integral component of the academic community, just as services such as an educational system or fire protection (professional or volunteer) are integral components of the crossroads community.

The academic library begins with collections, actual and virtual, just as crossroads begin with a literal crossing of pathways. These crossings are enhanced when a support system grows around them to fill community needs. In the same way, libraries are enhanced when they provide users with collections that are easy to use and relevant to their needs. Ultimately, tradition and common heritage sustain both crossroads community and academic library. Centrality, an important concept for the academic library, encompasses all of this—the success of users through services, access to collections, and tradition. As we look toward the twenty-first century, we must ensure that academic libraries and their users are not left stranded at forgotten crossroads; instead, we must develop academic libraries that are vibrant crossroads communities which truly meet the needs of all our users.

Notes

1. Judith Dozier Hackman, "Power and Peripherality: Developing a Practical Theory of Resources Allocation in Colleges and Universities" (Ph.D. diss., University of Michigan, Ann Arbor, 1983); Hanna Ashar, "Internal and Exter-

nal Variables and Their Effect on a University's Retrenchment Decisions: Two Theoretical Perspectives" (Ph.D. diss., University of Washington, 1987).

2. Using strategic contingencies theory, Gregory A. Crawford has also found that information technology is linked to intraorganizational power within the university and that libraries that have added more technologies have gained power in acquiring resources within the university. For specific information, see Gregory A. Crawford, "Information as a Strategic Contingency: Applying the Strategic Contingencies Theory of Intraorganizational Power to Academic Libraries," *College & Research Libraries* 58 (Mar. 1997): 145–55.

3. Quoted in Richard M. Dougherty and Ann P. Dougherty, "The Academic Library: A Time of Crisis, Change, and Opportunity," *Journal of Academic Librarianship* 18 (Jan. 1993): 344.

4. Although faculty members generally control course and program content, administrators generally determine which programs will be initiated, retained, supported, or eliminated.

5. Carla J. Stoffle, Robert Renaud, and Jerilyn R. Veldolf, "Choosing Our Futures," *College & Research Libraries* 57 (May 1996): 220.

6. The list of indicators includes *any* item mentioned positively by one or more of the interviewees. Nonindicators include items to which the interviewees responded negatively or noncommittally.

7. Descriptions of all EIs are given in appendix A, with emphases drawn from comments of the interviewees during the study. Although figures 10–12 have several EIs in common, the descriptions differentiate emphases between them, based on the focus of the figure (i.e., the concept).

8. Constance Ann Mellon, *Naturalistic Inquiry for Library Science: Methods and Applications for Research, Evaluation, and Teaching* (New York: Greenwood Pr., 1990); Jacqueline Fawcett and Florence S. Downs, *The Relationship of Theory and Research* (Norwalk, Conn.: Appleton-Century-Crofts, 1986).

9. Peter Hernon and Charles R. McClure, *Evaluation and Library Decision Making* (Norwalk, N.J.: Ablex, 1990), 155–70.

10. F. Wilfred Lancaster, *If You Want to Evaluate Your Library . . .* (Champaign, Ill.: Univ. of Illinois, Graduate School of Library and Information Science, 1988), 110–25.

11. Nancy A. Van House, Beth T. Weil, and Charles R. McClure, *Measuring Academic Library Performance: A Practical Approach* (Chicago: ALA, 1990), 83; see especially, pp. 82–88 and pp. 91–94.

12. Paul Metz, *The Landscape of Literatures: Use of Subject Collections in a University Library.* ACRL Publications in Librarianship, no. 43 (Chicago: American Library Association, 1983).

13. For specific examples, see Lancaster, *If You Want to Evaluation Your Library . . .*, 127–37, 20–21.

14. Ibid., 12.

15. Carol A. Hughes, "A Comparison of Perceptions and Campus Priorities: The 'Logical Library' in an Organized Anarchy," *Journal of Academic Librarianship* 18 (July 1992): 140.

16. Edward Shils, *Tradition* (Chicago: Univ. of Chicago Pr., 1981): 21.

17. Fawcett and Downs, *The Relationship of Theory and Research*, 21.

18. Quoted in Deborah Bloomfield, "The Agile Organization," *College & Research Libraries News* 57 (Apr. 1996): 202.

19. Van House, Weil, and McClure, *Measuring Academic Library Performance*, 7; see examples of use studies in Lancaster, *If You Want to Evaluate Your Library . . .*, 35–61, 60–70.

20. *Random House Webster's Electronic Dictionary and Thesaurus*, college ed.

21. Philip Tompkins, "New Structures in Teaching Libraries," *Library Administration & Management* 4 (spring 1990): 79.

22. For more information on the concept of the information commons, see Tompkins, "New Structures in Teaching Libraries"; Anita K. Lowry, "The Information Arcade at the University of Iowa," *CAUSE/Effect* 17 (fall 1994): 38–44; Deborah Holmes-Wong, Marianne Afifi, Shahla Bahavar, and Xioyang Liu, "If You Build It, They Will Come: Spaces, Values, and Services in the Digital Era," *Library Administration & Management* 11 (spring 1997): 74–85. See also Web sites for the University of Iowa, University of Southern California, and Maricopa County Community College District (respectively, http://www.lib.uiowa.edu/commons/info.html; http://www_lib.usc.edu/Info/Leavey/; and http:///www.mc.maricopa.edu/its/lib/.

23. ACRL, College Library Standards Committee, "Standards for University Libraries: Evaluation of Performance," *College & Research Libraries* 50 (Sept. 1989): 679.

24. Quoted in Bloomfield, "The Agile Organization," 202.

25. Irene B. Hoadley, Sheila Creth, and Herbert S. White, "Reactions to 'Defining the Academic Librarian,'" *College & Research Libraries* 46 (Nov. 1985): 469–77.

26. See various authors in the special theme issue of *Library Hi-Tech*, 11 (1993) for discussions on transaction log analysis.

27. Van House, Weil, and McClure, *Measuring Academic Library Performance*, General Satisfaction Form 1-1.

28. See, for example, John Lofland and Lyn H. Lofland, *Analyzing Social Settings: A Guide to Qualitative Observation and Analysis* (Belmont, Calif.: Wadsworth, 1984), 123; and Richard H. Brown, *A Poetic for Sociology: Toward a Logic of Discovery for the Human Sciences* (Cambridge: Cambridge Univ. Pr., 1977), 123.

29. Peter Lyman, "The Library of the (Not-So-Distant) Future," *Change* 23 (Jan./Feb. 1991): 40.

30. Dictionary definitions are drawn from *Random House Webster's Electronic Dictionary and Thesaurus*, college ed. [based on the Random House *Webster's College Dictionary*, 1992, and the *Random House Thesaurus*, college ed., 1984].

31. The sociological uses of metaphors are discussed in greater detail in chapter 1, with particular reference to the criteria offered by Brown in *A Poetic for Sociology* for evaluating metaphors as theory-building devices.

32. References are to *Oxford English Dictionary*, 1989 ed.

33. Tompkins, "New Structures in Teaching Libraries."

Appendix A
Interview Questions

Major Research Question 1A
What does the phrase, "The library is the heart of the university," mean, if anything, to you?

Follow-up Questions
Does this phrase equate with the mission of the academic library?

Do you believe that this is an accurate statement of the library's role on your campus? Should it be? Why or why not?

Major Research Question 1B
ACRL standards for university libraries state that centrality is an underlying assumption of the university library mission:

> The library is of central importance to the attainment of any university's goals. It is an organic combination of people, collections, and buildings, whose purpose is to assist users in the process of transforming information into knowledge.
>
> Information and knowledge are central to the attainment of any university's goals. The ways in which information is collected, stored, and distributed within the institution will, in large measure, determine the level and success of scholarship and knowledge.

Do you think this is an accurate statement?

Does it reflect reality on your campus?

Related Questions
Briefly, how is the university librarian or library director involved in university decision-making?

Does the library have a symbolic role on campus? Does this give it protected status in resource allocation decisions?

In what ways does the symbolic role show up? How does the library fulfill its symbolic role?

Major Research Question 2
Some institutions define centrality in terms of contributions to the mission and some in terms of connections between academic units? Which would you use?

Follow-up Question
What library resources or services do you consider critical to the university mission?

Related Questions
Some research relates control of uncertainty and critical resources or functions with power and centrality. Would you use any of these terms or concepts in regard to the library? In what ways?

Major Research Question 3
If we accept that the mission of the university as teaching, research, and service, is there a difference between the university's mission and its priorities?

How does the library contribute to the mission? In what observable ways?

How does the library contribute to the priorities? In what observable ways?

Follow-up Question

Under what conditions do library matters become a top priority? When do library matters become an emergency? How do you identify the emergency (i.e., how do you find out about it or decide that there is an emergency)?

Related Questions

At this institution, which is more important—teaching, research, or service? How does this affect the role that the library should be playing within the university?

Does the percentage of graduate to undergraduate students affect your view of the library's contributions to the university's mission? To its priorities?

Do you have a certain level of comfort or expectation about the library's contribution to the mission? If so, what do you examnine to determine if the library is meeting your expectations?

Does the amount of research conducted by academic units of the university affect your view of the library's contributions to the university's mission? To its priorities?

Major Research Question 4A

In your resource allocation decisions and retrenchment plan, what criteria do you apply to the library? Would you equate these with centrality?

Follow-up Question

What arguments are most cogent regarding library allocations?

Major Research Question 4B

Some research suggests that university administrators view what the faculty and students say about the library as more important than comparisons with other libraries. How do you feel about that?

Who on campus is most influential in your decisions regarding library allocations? Who outside the library?

Related Questions

Which of the following possible indicators do you believe are relevant to a library's centrality within the university:

> national prestige/reputation/ARL ranking
>
> involvement of librarians/library director in Faculty Senate or committee structure
>
> acquisition of outside funding
>
> research or paradigm development by library faculty/ personnel instructional or research collaborations
>
> quality of library personnel or collections
>
> campus visibility
>
> participation in high-level university decision-making
>
> service to other units of the institution
>
> substitutability vs. nonsubstitutability
>
> use? circulation statistics? ILL statistics?
>
> proportion of graduates to undergraduates
>
> innovation/creativity
>
> relationship with other universities
>
> program costs
>
> geographic uniqueness
>
> symbolic vs. practical roles

Wrap-up Questions

What makes you most proud of the library? What makes you least proud?

How has the library or library director helped you in your work recently?

Is there anything else you would like to comment on or to add?

Appendix B
Descriptions of Indicators of Academic Library Centrality

All descriptions are drawn from the comments of interviewees and their responses to interview questions.

Empirical Indicators (EIs) from Figure 10. General Indicators of Academic Library Centrality

EI1: *Geographic uniqueness*: Refers to the uniqueness of the library in its geographic area; related to urban/rural nature of university and proximity to other teaching or research centers.

EI2: *Quality and expertise of personnel*: Refers to the capabilities of the librarians and/or library staff to identify and provide the services needed by library users; related to expertise in identifying and providing access to external sources of information via information technology.

EI3: *Community or external support, including alumni support*: Refers to the formal and informal means through which members of the local community and broader community in which the university resides express their views on the services, resources, and facilities provided by the campus library; refers also to financial support provided by alumni.

EI14: *Current reputation or prestige of the library*: Refers to the reputation of an academic department, also to the reputation or official ARL ranking of the campus library.

EI5: *History of reputation or excellence of the library, including ARL ranking*: Refers to long-standing reputation held by the academic department, also to the reputation of the library in providing an excellent research collection; refers also to ARL ranking (which requires time to develop and effort to maintain over time).

EI6: *Uniqueness of services offered (i.e., criticality and substitutability)* Refers to the services, resources, or facilities provided by the campus library that are not available through other means. Substitutability refers to alternate means by which information is acquired or provided, such as departmental databases.

EI7: *Number of people affected, including number of graduate students (i.e., use)*: Refers to the number of users served by the campus library, including the size of the graduate student population; reflected in circulation statistics, interlibrary loan statistics, and so forth (although statistics alone are not considered indicative of library centrality).

EI8: *Symbolic role*: Refers to the emphasis placed on the symbolic role of the library as related to the university mission (further discussed in text).

EI9: *Information storage and retrieval*: Refers to the traditional role of the library.

EI10: *Service attitude/responsiveness of library personnel*: Refers to the approach taken by librarians or library staff in providing services and to their responsiveness to user requests.

EI11: *Faculty and student opinion*: Refers to both formal and informal means through which faculty and students express their views on the services, resources, and facilities provided by the library.

EI12: *Quality and reputation of the university*: Refers to the quality and reputation of the university, regardless of the quality/reputation of the library; also related to the quality of the library and to ARL ranking.

EI13: *Providing good information about the library to the CEOs/CAOs*: Refers to the information provided by the CLO to the CAO and CEO about the campus library, information technologies, scholarly communication, and changes in any of these.

EI14: *Speed of responses and acquisition of information*: Refers to the speed with which library users can expect to receive the information they seek, either in the campus library or through access to other sources.

EI15: *Access to information and mechanisms for access, including current level of technology*: Refers to the provision of, or mechanisms for, access to sources of information, regardless of the location of either the user or the information.

EI16: *Convenience to users*: Refers to the ease and timeliness with which users may expect to locate and retrieve the information they seek; also related to EI2 and EI10; also related to facilities and services.

EI17: *Size and quality of the library's collection, including periodicals*: Refers to the number and quality of library resources on campus in support of teaching and research; includes, in particular, periodicals and current scholarly materials required for research.

EI18: *Specific services offered by the library*: Refers to the specific services offered by the library to support the mission of the university; related to the uniqueness of services available on campus to help students and faculty locate and acquire information; related to almost all the indicators in this figure.

EI19: *Practical role and use of the library*: Refers to the actual uses made of the library by all users; related to circulation and interlibrary loan statistics (although statistics alone are not considered to be indicative of library centrality).

EI20: *Quality of facilities provided by the library, including the provision of study hall space and a warm environment*: Refers to both the physical facilities and its appeal to students; considered important in attracting undergraduates, in particular, to use the library for study or research.

EI21: *University priorities (i.e., research priorities are linked to library collections and services); development and growth of research disciplines;*

specific inclusion of the library in plans to improve programs: Refers to the priorities established by the university in regard to teaching (especially undergraduate education); refers to library support needed for the growth an development of disciplines and to specific planning to include library support as plans are made to improve instructional programs.

Empirical Indicators (EIs) from Figure 11. Indicators of Academic Library Centrality Related to the Research Component of the University Mission

EI1: *Size and quality of the library's collection, including periodicals*: Refers to the number and quality of library resources available on campus in support of graduate instruction and research. Especially important for research are current periodicals and/or access to sources of current information for faculty and graduate-level research.

EI2: *Specific services offered by the library*: Refers to the specific services offered by the library in support of graduate education; related to almost all the indicators in this figure.

EI3: *Practical role and use of the library*: Refers to the actual uses made of the library in undergraduate education; related to circulation and interlibrary loan statistics (although statistics alone are not considered to be indicative of library centrality).

EI4: *Faculty and student opinion*: Refers to the formal and informal means through which students and faculty express their views on services, facilities, and resources provided by the campus library.

EI5: *Quality and expertise of library personnel*: Refers to the capabilities of the librarians and/or library staff to identify and provide the services needed by library users; related to ability of personnel to help researchers locate and use information sources.

EI6: *Quality and reputation of the university*: Refers to overall quality of the university and its instructional and research programs. Interviewees expected a university of good reputation to have a library of good reputation.

EI7: *Information storage and retrieval*: Refers to the traditional role of the library.

EI8: *University priorities (especially the development and growth of research disciplines); specific inclusion of the library in plans to improve programs*: Refers to the priorities established by the university in regard to research; refers to library support needed for the growth and development of disciplines and to specific planning to include library support as plans are made to improve instructional programs.

EI9: *Providing good information about the library to the CEOs/CAOs*: Refers to the information provided by the CLO to the CAO or CEO about the campus library, information technologies, scholarly communication, and changes in any of these.

EI10: *Speed of responses and acquisition of information*: Refers to the speed with which library users can expect to receive the information they seek, either in the campus library or through access to other sources. Speed is especially important to researchers who have little time and/or need to be competitive in their research.

EI11: *Access to information and mechanisms for access, including periodicals*: Refers to the provision of, or mechanisms for, access to sources of information, regardless of the location of either the user or the information; especially important to researchers.

EI12: *Geographic uniqueness*: Refers to the uniqueness of the library in its geographic area; related to urban/rural nature of university and proximity to other research centers.

EI13: *Uniqueness of services offered (i.e., criticality and substitutability)*: Refers to the services, resources, or facilities provided by the campus library that are not available through other means. Substitutability refers to alternate means by which information is acquired or provided, such as departmental databases.

EI14: *Community or external financial support, including alumni support*: Refers to the formal and informal means through which members of the local community and broader community in which the university resides express their views on the services, resources, and facilities provided by the campus library; refers also to financial support provided by alumni.

EI5: *Current reputation or prestige of the library*: Refers to the reputation of an academic department; also to the reputation or official ARL ranking of the campus library; important in securing research grants and recruiting researchers, students, and faculty.

EI6: *History of reputation or excellence of the library, including ARL ranking*: Refers to long-standing reputation held by the academic department, also to the reputation of the library in providing an excellent research collection; refers also to ARL ranking (which requires time to develop and effort to maintain over time); important in securing research grants and recruiting researchers, students, and faculty; related to external and alumni financial support.

EI7: *Number of people affected, especially graduate students (i.e., use)*: Refers to the number of users served by the campus library, including the size the graduate student population (who will put greater demands on library services than undergraduates); reflected in circulation statistics, interlibrary loan statistics, and so forth (although statistics alone are not considered indicative of library centrality).

EI8: *Symbolic role*: Refers to the emphasis placed on the symbolic role of the library as related to the university mission (further discussed in text).

Empirical Indicators (EIs) from Figure 12. Indicators of Academic Library Centrality Related to the Teaching Component of the University Mission

EI1: *Size and quality of the library's collection, including periodicals*: Refers to the number and quality of library resources available on campus in support of undergraduate instruction; also related to university priorities for instruction and growth of disciplines.

EI2: *Specific services offered by the library*: Refers to the specific services offered by the library in support of undergraduate education; related to almost all the indicators in this figure.

EI3: *Practical role and use of the library*: Refers to the actual uses made of the library in undergraduate education; related to circulation and interlibrary loan statistics (although statistics alone are not considered to be indicative of library centrality).

EI4: *Faculty and (especially) student opinion*: Refers to the formal and informal means through which undergraduates express their views on the services, facilities, and resources provided by the campus library; viewed as especially important for undergraduate students.

EI5: *Quality and expertise of personnel*: Refers to the capabilities of the librarians and/or library staff to identify and provide the services needed by library users; related to ability of personnel to help undergraduates locate and use information sources.

EI6: *Quality and reputation of the university*: Refers to overall quality of the university and its instructional and research programs. Interviewees expected a university of good reputation to have a library of good reputation.

EI7: *Information storage and retrieval* : Refers to the traditional role of the library.

EI8: *University priorities (especially the development and growth of disciplines); specific inclusion of the library in plans to improve programs*: Refers to the priorities established by the university in regard to teaching (especially undergraduate education); refers to library support needed for the growth and development of disciplines and to specific planning to include library support as plans are made to improve instructional programs.

EI9: *Providing good information about the library to the CEOs/CAOs*: Refers to the information provided by the CLO to the CAO or CEO about the campus library, information technologies, scholarly communication, and changes in any of these.

EI10: *Speed of responses and acquisition of information*: Refers to the speed with which library users can expect to receive the information they seek, either in the campus library or through access to other sources. Undergraduates tend to delay research and work requiring library resources, so speed is important because they allot little time for this activity.

EI11: *Access to information and mechanisms for access, including current level of technology*: Refers to the provision of, or mechanisms for, access to sources of information, regardless of the location of either the user or the information.

EI12: *Quality of library facilities (especially including the provision of study space and a warm environment)*: Refers to the general condition of library facilities, including floor space and amount of study seating. Interviewees pointed out that undergraduates are looking for comfortable and suitable study hall space and a welcoming environment.

EI13: *Service attitude or responsiveness of library personnel*: Refers to the approach taken by librarians and library staff in providing services and assistance to undergraduates; related to librarians' skills and expertise.

EI14: *Convenience to users*: Refers to the ease and timeliness with which users may expect to locate and retrieve the information they seek; also related to the attitude and expertise of staff and opinions of users.

Bibliography

Allen, Frank R., and Sarah Barbara Watstein. "Point/Counterpoint: The Value of Place." *College & Research Libraries News* 57 (June 1996): 372–73.

Allen, Nancy, and James F. Williams III. "Managing Technology: Innovation: Who's in Charge Here?" *Journal of Academic Librarianship* 20 (July 1994): 167–68.

Allen, Robert W., and Lyman W. Porter. *Organizational Influence Processes*. Glenview, Ill.: Scott, Foresman, 1983.

America 2000: An Education Strategy: A Sourcebook. Washington, D.C.: U.S. Department of Education, 1991.

American Library Directory 1989–90. 42nd. ed. Chicago: ALA, 1989.

American Universities and Colleges. 134th ed. New York: Bowker, 1989.

Arendt, Hannah. *On Violence*. San Diego, Calif.: Harcourt, Brace, Jovanovich, 1970.

Ashar, Hanna. "Internal and External Variables and Their Effect on a University's Retrenchment Decisions: Two Theoretical Perspectives." Ph.D. diss., University of Washington, 1987.

Ashar, Hanna, and Johnathan Z. Shapiro. Measuring Centrality: A Note on Hackman's Resource Allocation Theory. *Administrative Science Quarterly* 33 (June 1988): 275–83.

Association of College and Research Libraries, College Library Standards Committee. Standards for University Libraries: Evaluation of Performance, *College & Research Libraries* 50 (Sept. 1989): 679–91.

Auld, Douglas A. L., Graham Bannock, R.E. Baxter, and Ray Rees. *The American Dictionary of Economics*. New York: Facts on File, 1983. S.v. "Budget."

Bailey, Kenneth D. *Methods of Social Research*. 3rd. ed. New York: Free Press, 1987.

Baldridge, J. Victor, David V. Curtis, George P. Ecker, and Gary L. Riley. "Alternative Models of Governance in Higher Education." In *Governing Academic Organizations*, edited by J. Victor Baldridge and Terrence E. Deal, 22–25. (Berkeley, Calif.: McCutchan, 1977). Reprinted in *ASHE Reader on Organization and Governance in Higher Education*, 3rd. ed., edited by Marvin W. Peterson, 11–35. Lexington, Mass.: Ginn Press, 1986.

Baltes, Paula Choate. "Toward a Theory of Retrenchment in Higher Education." Ph.D. diss., University of Arizona, 1985.

Bell, Edwin Dewey. "Some Theoretical Implications of Power, Resource Allocation, and Theories of Action in Higher Education." Ed.D. diss., University of North Carolina at Greenville, 1985.

Ben-David, Joseph. *Centers of Learning: Britain, France, Germany, United States*. New York: McGraw-Hill, 1977.

Bertalanffy, Ludwig von. *General Systems Theory: Foundations, Development, Applications*. New York: G. Braziller, 1968.

Black, Max. *Models and Metaphors: Studies in Language and Philosophy*. Ithaca, N.Y.: Cornell University Press, 1962.

Bloomfield, Deborah. "The Agile Organization." *College & Research Libraries News* 57 (Apr. 1996): 201–2.

Bloomfield, Stefan D. "Analytical Tools for Budget Reductions: A Case Study." Paper presented at 24th Annual Forum of the Association for Institutional Research, Fort Worth, Tex., May 6–9, 1984. ERIC ED 246 790.

Boyer, Ernest L. *College: The Undergraduate Experience in America*. New York: Harper & Row, 1987.

Brown, Richard H. *A Poetic for Sociology: Toward a Logic of Discovery for the Human Sciences*. Cambridge: Cambridge University Press, 1977.

Buck, Paul H. *Libraries and Universities; Addresses and Reports*. Cambridge, Mass.: Belknap Press of Harvard University Press, 1964.

Budd, John, and Patricia Coutant. *Faculty Perceptions of Librarians: A Survey*, 1981. ERIC ED 215 697.

Burns, Tom, and G. M. Stalker. *The Management of Innovation*. London: Tavistock Press, 1961.

Caruso, Annette Carolyn. "Implementing Program Review: An Analysis of the Graduate Program Review Process at the Pennsylvania State University." Ed.D. diss., Pennsylvania State University, 1985.

Ceppos, Karen Feingold. "Innovation and Survival in Library Education." Ph.D. diss., University of California, 1989.

Chabotar, Kent John, and James P. Honan. "Coping with Retrenchment: Strategies and Tactics." *Change* 22 (Nov./Dec. 1990): 28–34.

Chaffee, Ellen Earle. "Decision Models in University Budgeting." Ph.D. diss., Stanford University, 1981.

Cohen, Irit, and Ran Lachman. "The Generality of the Strategic Contingencies Approach to Subunit Power." *Organization Studies* 9 (Oct. 1988): 371–91.

Cohen, M.D., and J.G. March. *Leadership and Ambiguity*. New York: McGraw-Hill, 1974.

Cohen, M. D., J. G. March, and J. P. Olsen. "A Garbage Can Model of Organizational Choice." *Administrative Science Quarterly* 17 (Mar. 1972): 1–25.

Collins, Lyndhurst. *The Use of Models in the Social Sciences*. Boulder, Colo.: Tavistock Press, 1976.

Cook, M. Kathy. "Rank, Status, and Contributions of Academic Librarians As Perceived by Teaching Faculty at Southern Illinois University, Carbondale." *College & Research Libraries* 42 (May 1981): 214–23.

Cooper, Lloyd G. "The Politics of Retrenchment in Higher Education." Paper presented at the National Conference of Professors of Educational Administration, San Marcos, Tex., August 15–20, 1980. ERIC ED 225–500.

Cooper, Marianne, and Shoshana Kaufman. "Library Schools and Their Host Academic Libraries: Relationships, Power, Perceptions." *Journal of Academic Librarianship* 16 (Mar. 1990): 27–34.

Crawford, Gregory A. "Information as a Strategic Contingency: Applying the Strategic Contingencies Theory of Intraorganizational Power to Academic Libraries." *College & Research Libraries* 56 (Mar. 1997): 145–56.

Crawford, Walt, and Michael Gorman. *Future Libraries: Dreams, Madness, & Reality*. Chicago: ALA, 1995.

Crowley, Bill. "Redefining the Status of the Librarian." *College & Research Libraries* 57 (Mar. 1996): 113–21.

Crozier, Michel. *The Bureaucratic Phenomenon*. Chicago: University of Chicago Press, 1964.

Cummings, Anthony M., Marcia L. White, William G. Bowler, Laura O. Lazarus, and Richard H. Ekman. *University Libraries and Schol-*

arly Communication: A Study Prepared for the Andrew W. Mellon Foundation. Washington, D.C.: ARL, 1992.

Cummings, Martin M. *The Economics of Research Libraries*. Washington, D.C.: Council on Library Resources, 1986.

Cutter, Charles Ammi. *Rules for a Printed Dictionary Catalogue*. Washington, D.C.: U. S. Bureau of Education, 1876.

Cyert, R. M., and James G. March. "A Behavioral Theory of Organizational Objectives." In *Modern Organization Theory*, edited by M. Haire (New York: Wiley, 1959). Reprinted in Jay M. Shafritz and J. Steven Ott, *Classics of Organization Theory*. 2nd ed., rev. and expanded (Pacific Grove, Calif.: Brooks/Cole), 1987, 155–65.

———. *A Behavioral Theory of the Firm*. Englewood Cliffs, N.J.: Prentice-Hall, 1963.

Davis, Otto A., M.A.H. Dempster, and Aaron Wildawsky. "A Theory of the Budgetary Process." *American Political Science Review* 60 (Sept. 1966): 529–47.

Deighton, Lee C., ed. *Encyclopedia of Education*. New York: Macmillan and the Free Press, 1971. S.v. "Universities, history of," by Robert L. Church.

Divay, Gaby, Ada M. Ducas, and Nicole Michaud-Oystryk. "Faculty Perceptions of Librarians at the University of Manitoba." *College & Research Libraries* 48 (Jan. 1987): 27–35.

Dougherty, Richard M., and Ann P. Dougherty. "The Academic Library: A Time of Crisis, Change, and Opportunity." *Journal of Academic Librarianship* 18 (Jan. 1993): 342–46.

Dube, C. Stuart II, and Albert W. Brown. "Strategic Assessment—A Rational Response to University Cutbacks." *Long-Range Planning* 16 (Apr. 1983): 105–13.

Euster, Joanne R. "The Academic Library: Its Place and Role in the Institution." In *Academic Libraries: Their Rationale and Role in American Higher Education*, edited by Gerard B. McCabe and Ruth J. Person, 1–13. Westport, Conn.: Greenwood Press, 1995.

Fawcett, Jacquieline, and Florence S. Downs. *The Relationship of Theory and Research*. Norwalk, Conn.: Appleton-Century-Crofts, 1986.

Fiske, Edward B. *Selective Guide to Colleges*. 3rd. ed. New York: Times Books, 1985.

Flower, Kenneth E., ed. "Academic Libraries on the Periphery: How Telecommunications Information Policy is Determined in Universities."

Occasional Paper No. 11. Washington, D.C.: ARL, Office of Management Studies, 1986.

Fried, Bruce J. "Power Acquisition in a Health Care Setting: An Application of Strategic Contingencies Theory." *Human Relations* 42 (Dec. 1988): 915–27.

Galbraith, Jay. *Designing Complex Organizations*. Reading, Mass.: Academic Press, 1973

Garvin, David A. *The Economics of University Behavior*. New York: Academic Press, 1980.

Gaughan, Tom. "Taking the Pulse of Library Education. Part I." *American Libraries* 22 (Dec. 1991): 1020–21+.

———. "Taking the Pulse of Library Education. Part II." *American Libraries* 23 (Jan. 1992): 24–25.

Geiger, Roger L. *To Advance Knowledge: The Growth of American Research Universities, 1900–1940*. New York: Oxford University Press, 1986.

Georgiou. P. "The Goal Paradigm and Notes toward a Counter Paradigm." *Administrative Science Quarterly* 18 (Sep. 1973): 291–310.

Grimes, Deborah Jeanne. "Centrality and the Academic Library." Ph.D. diss., University of Alabama, 1993.

Hackman, Judith Dozier. "Power and Centrality in the Allocation of Resources in Colleges and Universities." *Administrative Science Quarterly* 30 (Mar. 1985): 61–77.

———. "Power and Peripherality: Developing a Practical Theory of Resources Allocation in Colleges and Universities." Ph.D. diss., University of Michigan, Ann Arbor, 1983.

Hamlin, Arthur T. *The University Library in the United States: Its Origin and Development*. Philadelphia: University of Pennsylvania Press, 1981.

Hardesty, Larry L. *Faculty and the Library: The Undergraduate Experience*. Norwood, N.J.: Ablex, 1991.

Hardesty, Larry L., and David Kaser. "What Do Academic Administrators Think about the Library? A Summary Report to the Council on Library Resources, Grant CLR 8018-A, Feb. 1990. Photocopy.

Hart, Peyton. "Principles and Standards for Surveying a College Library." *College & Research Libraries* 2 (Dec. 1940): 110–16.

Heim, Kathleen M., and J. Keith Ostertag. "Sources of Institutional Power: An Analysis of Faculty Policy Participation as an Agent of Influence and Domain." *Library Quarterly* 61 (Jul. 1991): 282–92.

Hernon, Peter, and Charles R. McClure. *Evaluation and Library Decision-Making.* Norwood, N.J.: Ablex, 1990.

Heydinger, Richard P. *Using Program Priorities to Make Retrenchment Decisions: The Case of the University of Minnesota.* Atlanta: Southern Regional Education Board, 1983. ERIC ED 230 119.

Hickson, D. J., C. R. Hinings, C. A. Lee, R. E. Schneck, and J. M. Pennings. "A 'Strategic Contingencies' Theory of Intraorganizational Power." *Administrative Science Quarterly* 16 (JunE 1971): 216–29.

Hills, Frederick S., and Thomas A. Mahoney. "University Budgets and Organizational Decision-Making." *Administrative Science Quarterly* 23 (Sept. 1978): 454–65.

Hinings, C. R., D. J. Hickson, J. M. Pennings, and R. E. Schneck. "Structural Conditions of Intraorganizational Power." *Administrative Science Quarterly* 19 (Mar. 1974): 22–44.

Hoadley, Irene B., Sheila Creth, and Herbert S. White. "Reactions to 'Defining the Academic Librarian.'" *College & Research Libraries* 46 (Nov. 1985): 309–19.

Holmes-Wang, Deborah, Marianne Afiti, Shahla Bahavar, and Xioyang Liu. "If You Build It, They Will Come: Spaces, Values, and Services in the Digital Era." *Library Administration & Management* 11 (spring 1997): 74–85.

Hopkins, Frances. "Bibliographic Instruction: An Emerging Professional Discipline." In *Directions for the Decade: Library Instruction for the 1980s,* edited by Carolyn A. Kirkendall, 13–24. Ann Arbor, Mich.: Pierian, 1981.

Howard, Helen A. "Organization Theory and Its Applications in Research in Librarianship." *Library Trends* 22 (spring 1984): 477–93.

Hubbard, Abigail. "Structural Power and Resource Allocation in the Multicampus University System." Ph.D. diss., University of Nebraska, 1983.

Huff, Sid. "Power and the Information Systems Department." *Business Quarterly* 55 (winter 1991): 50–53.

Hughes, Carol A. "A Comparison of Perceptions and Campus Priorities: The 'Logical' Library in an Organized Anarchy." *Journal of Academic Librarianship* 18 (July 1992): 140–45.

Hyatt, James A., and Aurora S. Santiago. *University Libraries in Transition.* Washington, D.C.: National Association of College and University Business Officers, 1987.

Hyatt, James., Carol Hernstadt Shulman, and Aurora S. Santiago. *Strategies for Effective Resource Management*. Washington, D.C.: National Association of College and University Business Officers, 1984.

Ikenberry, Stanley O., and Renee C. Friedman. *Beyond Academic Departments*. 2nd. ed. New York: Wiley & Sons, 1972.

Jacobson, Trudi E., and John R. Vallely. "The Half-Built Bridge: The Unfinished Work of Bibliographic Instruction." *Journal of Academic Librarianship* 17 (Jan. 1992): 359–63.

Katz, Daniel, and Robert L. Kahn. *The Social Psychology of Organizations*. New York: Wiley, 1966.

Katzer, Jeffrey. "A Lesson to Be Learned." *Library Quarterly* 61 (Jul. 1991): 291–92.

Keresztesi, Michael. "The Science of Bibliography: Theoretical Implications for Bibliographic Instruction." In *Theories of Bibliographic Education: Designs for Teaching*, edited by Cerise Oberman and Katina Strauch, 1–26. New York: Bowker, 1982.

Kingma, Bruce R., and Gillian M. McCombs. "The Opportunity Costs of Faculty Status for Academic Librarians." *College & Research Libraries* 56 (May 1995): 258–64.

Kotter, John. *Power and Influence: Beyond Formal Authority*. New York: Free Press, 1985.

Lachman, Ran. "Power from What? A Re-examination of Its Relationships with Structural Conditions." *Administrative Science Quarterly* 34 (June 1989): 97–105.

Ladd, Dwight R. "Myths and Realities of University Governance." *College & Research Libraries* 36 (Mar. 1975): 97–105.

Lancaster, F. Wilfred. *If You Want to Evaluate Your Library . . . .* Champagne, Ill.: University of Illinois, 1988.

Lawrence, Paul R., and Jay W. Lorsch. "Organization–Environment Interface." In *Developing Organizations: Diagnosis and Action* Reading, Mass.: Addison, Wesley, 1969. Reprinted in Jay M. Shafritz and J. Steven Ott, *Classics of Organization Theory*. 2nd ed., rev. and expanded. Pacific Grove, Calif.: Brooks/Cole, 1987, 205–9.

Library Hi-Tech 11 (spring 1993). Special theme issue. Various authors.

Lincoln, Yvonna S., and Jane Tuttle. "Centrality as a Prior Criterion." Paper presented at the Joint Meeting of the Association for the Study of Higher Education and the American Educational Research Association, Division J, San Francisco, Oct. 19–21, 1983. ERIC ED 240 934.

Lofland, John, and Lyn H. Lofland. *Analyzing Social Settings: A Guide to Qualitative Observation and Analysis*. Belmont, Calif.: University of California, 1984.

Lowry, Anita K. "The Information Arcade at the University of Iowa." *CAUSE/Effect* 17 (fall 1994): 38–44.

Lozier, G. Gregory, and P. Richard Althouse. "Supporting Quality through Priority Setting and Reallocation." Paper presented at 22nd. Annual Forum of the Association for Institutional Research, Denver, Colo., May 16–19, 1982. ERIC ED 220 053.

Lyman, Peter. "The Library of the (Not-So-Distant) Future." *Change* (Jan./Feb. 1991): 35–41.

March, J. G., and Herbert A. Simon. *Organizations*. New York: Wiley, 1958.

Martin, Lowell A. *Organizational Structure of Libraries*. Metuchen, N.J.: Scarecrow, 1984.

Martin, Susan K. "Information Technology and Libraries: Toward the Year 2000." *College & Research Libraries* 50 (July 1989): 397–405.

McAnally, Arthur M., and Robert B. Downs. "The Changing Roles of Directors of University Libraries." *College & Research Libraries* 34 (Mar. 1973): 103–25.

McCune, Ellis E. "Resource Allocations at California State University, Hayward." In *Organizational Structure of Libraries*, edited by Lowell A. Martin, 26–35. (Metuchen, N.J.: Scarecrow, 1984).

Melchiori, Gerlinda S. *Planning for Program Discontinuance: From Default to Design*. AAHE-ERIC/Higher Education Research Report No. 5. New York: Exxon Education Foundation; Ann Arbor, Mich.: Michigan University, National Institute of Education, 1982. ERIC ED 224 451.

Mellon, Constance Ann. *Naturalistic Inquiry for Library Science: Methods and Applications for Research, Evaluation, and Teaching*. New York: Greenwood Press, 1990.

Metz, Paul. *The Landscape of Literatures: Use of Subject Collections in a University Library*. Chicago: ALA, 1983.

Miles, Matthew B., and A. Michael Huberman. *Qualitative Analysis: A Sourcebook of New Methods*. Beverly Hills, Calif.: Sage, 1984.

Mintzberg, Henry. *Mintzberg on Management: Inside Our Strange World of Organizations*. New York: Free Press, 1989.

Moffett, William A. Guest Editorial: "Talking to Ourselves." *College & Research Libraries* 50 (Nov. 1989): 609–10.

Mortimer, Kenneth P., and Michael L. Tierney. *The Three "R's" of the Eighties: Reduction, Reallocation, and Retrenchment.* AAHE/Higher Education Research Report No. 4. Washington, D.C.: American Association for Higher Education, 1979.

Munn, Robert F. "The Bottomless Pit, or the Academic Library as Viewed from the Administration Building." *College & Research Libraries* 29 (Jan. 1968) 51–54. Reprinted in *College & Research Libraries* 50 (Nov. 1968): 635–37 (page references are to reprint edition).

National Institute of Education, Study Group on the Conditions of Excellence in American Higher Education. *Involvement in Learning: Realizing the Potential of American Higher Education.* Washington, D.C.: National Institute of Education, 1991.

Odi, Amusi. "Creative Research and Theory Building in Library and Information Sciences." *College & Research Libraries* 43 (July 1982): 312–19.

O'Neill, Robert M. "Academic Libraries and the Future: A President's View." *College & Research Libraries* 47 (May 1986): 184–93.

The Oxford English dictionary. 1989 ed. S.v. "Crossroad."

The Oxford English dictionary. 1989 ed. S.v. "Heart."

Paris, Marion. "Library School Closings: Four Case Studies." Ph.D. diss., Indiana University, 1986.

Parson, Willie L. "User Perception on a New Paradigm for Librarianship." *College & Research Libraries* 45 (Sept. 1984): 370–73.

Parsons, Talcott. "Suggestions for a Sociological Approach to the Theory of Organizations." *Administrative Science Quarterly* 1 (1956): 63–85. Reprinted in Jay M. Shafritz and J. Steven Ott, *Classics of Organization Theory.* 2nd. ed., rev. and expanded. Pacific Grove, Calif.: Brooks/Cole, 1987, 132–46.

Perrow, Charles. "The Short and Glorious History of Organization Theory." In *Creative Organization Theory: A Resource Book*, edited by Gareth Morgan, 41–48. Newbury Park, Calif.: Sage, 1973.

Perry, John, and Anne Woodsworth. "Managing Technology: Innovation and Change: Can We Learn from Corporate Models?" *Journal of Academic Librarianship* 20 (Mar. 1995): 117–20.

Peters, Thomas A., Martin Kurth, and Patricia Flaherty. "Special Theme: Transaction Log Analysis." *Library Hi-Tech* 11 (spring 1993): 37–40.

Pfeffer, Jeffrey. "Understanding the Role of Decision-Making." In *Power in Organizations,* 21–31. Marshfield, Mass.: Pitman, 1981. Reprinted in Jay M. Shafritz and J. Steven Ott, *Classics of Organization Theory*, 2nd ed., rev. and expanded. Pacific Grove, Calif.: Brooks/Cole, 1987, 309–44.

Pfeffer, Jeffrey, and Gerald R. Salancik. "Organizational Decision-Making as a Political Process: The Case of the University Budget." *Administrative Science Quarterly* 19 (June 1974): 135–51.

Pitkin, Gary M., ed. *Information Management and Organizational Change in Higher Education.* Westport, Conn.: Meckler, 1992.

Polidoro, J. Richard. *Rebalancing the University: Will Physical Education Survive?* Kingston, R. I., University of Rhode Island, 1983. ERIC ED 235 126.

Pritchard, Sara M. 1991. Memorandum to directors of ARL libraries, April 22, 1991.

———. Memorandum to Directors of ARL Libraries. Jan. 21, 1992

Project on Redefining the Meaning and Purpose of the Baccalaureate Degree. *Integrity in the College Curriculum: A Report to the Academic Community.* Washington, D.C.: Association of American Colleges, 1985.

Provan, Keith G. "Environment, Department Power, and Strategic Decision-Making in Organizations: A Proposed Integration." *Journal of Management* 15 (Mar. 1989): 21–34.

Raffel, Lee, and Robert Shishko. *Systematic Analysis of University Libraries: An Application of Cost-Benefit Analysis of the M.I.T. Libraries.* Cambridge: M.I.T. Press, 1979.

Random House Webster's Electronic Dictionary and Thesaurus. College ed. Based on the Random House *Webster's College Dictionary*, 1991, and the Random House Thesaurus, College Edition, 1984. S.v. "Community."

———. ———. S.v. "Crossroad."

Rayward, W. Boyd. "Libraries as Organizations." *College & Research Libraries* 30 (July 1969): 312–26.

Riley, Gresham. "Myths and Realities: The Academic Viewpoint II." *College & Research Libraries* 45 (Sept. 1984): 367–69.

Salancik, Gerald R., and Jeffrey Pfeffer. "The Bases and Uses of Power in Organizational Decision-Making: The Case of the University." *Administrative Science Quarterly* 19 (Dec. 1974): 453–73.

Saunders, Carol S., and Richard Scamell. "Intraorganizational Distributions of Power: Replication Research." *Academy of Management Journal* 25 (Mar. 1982): 192–200.

Scott, William G. "Organization Theory: A Reassessment." *Academy of Management Journal* 17 (June 1974): 242–54.

Shafritz, Jay M., and J. Steven Ott. *Classics of Organization Theory*. 2nd. ed., rev. and expanded. Pacific Grove, Calif.: Brooks/Cole, 1987.

Shils, Edward. *Tradition*. Chicago: University of Chicago Press, 1981.

Sils, David, ed. *International Encyclopedia of the Social Sciences*. New York: Macmillan Co. and Free Press, 1968. S.v. "Power," by Robert A. Dahl.

Simon, Herbert A. "The Proverbs of Administration." *Public Administration Review* 6 (winter 1946): 53–67.

Slattery, Charles E. "Faculty Status: Another 100 Years of Dialogue? Lessons from the Library School Closings." *Journal of Academic Librarianship* 20 (Sept. 1994): 193–94.

Smith, Kenwyn K., and Valerie M. Simmons. "A Rumpelstiltskin Organization: Metaphors on Metaphors in Field Research." *Administrative Science Quarterly* 28 (Sept. 1983): 377–92.

Stieg, Margaret F. "The Closing of Library Schools: Darwinism at the University." *Library Quarterly* 62 (July 1991): 266–72.

Stoffle, Carla J., Robert Renaud, and Jerily R. Veldolf. "Choosing Our Futures." *College & Research Libraries* 57 (May 1996): 215–25.

Thompson James D. *Organizations in Action*. New York: McGraw-Hill, 1967.

Tompkins, Philip. "New Structures in Teaching Libraries." *Library Administration & Management* (spring 1990): 77–81.

U.S. Bureau of Education. *Public Libraries in the United States: Their History, Condition, and Management.* Washington, D.C.: Department of the Interior, 1876. Special Report.

U.S. Department of Education. *Alliance for Excellence: Librarians Respond to "A Nation at Risk"*. Washington, D.C.: Government Printing Office, 1984.

———. *America 2000: An Education Strategy: Sourcebook*. Washington, DC: Goverment Printing Office, 1991.

U.S. National Commission on Excellence in Education. *A Nation at Risk: The Imperative for Educational Reform*. Washington, D.C.: Government Printing Office, 1983.

Van House, Nancy A., Beth T. Weil, and Charles R. McClure. *Measuring Academic Library Performance: A Practical Approach*. Chicago, ALA, 1990.

Veaner, Allen B. "1985 to 1995: The Next Decade of Academic Librarianship, Part I." *College & Research Libraries* 46 (May 1985): 209–29.

Walker, A.H., and J.W. Lorsch. "Organizational Choice: Product vs. Function." *Harvard Business Review* 46 (Nov./Dec. 1968): 129–38.

Weick, Karl E. "Organizational Design. Organizations as Self-Designing Systems." *Organizational Dynamics* 6 (autumn 1977): 30–46.

———. *The Social Psychology of Organizing.* Reading, Mass.: Addison-Wesley, 1979.

Weiner, Norbert. *Cybernetics.* Cambridge, Mass.: M.I.T. Press, 1948.

White, Herbert S. "Politics, the World We Live In." *Library Quarterly* 61 (July 1991): 262–66.

Wilson, Logan. "Library Roles in American Higher Education." *College & Research Libraries* 31 (Mar. 1970): 96–102.

Wilson, Robert A., ed. "Allocating and Reallocating Financial Resources in an Environment of Fiscal Stress." Topical Paper No. 24. *Selected Proceedings of the Annual Conference on Higher Education* (Tuscon, Ariz.: University of Arizona, 1984). ERIC ED 251 025.

Woodsworth, Anne. "Getting Off the Library Merry-Go-Round: McAnally and Downs Revisited." *Library Journal* 114 (May 1989): 35–38.

Zammuto, Raymond F. "Managing Decline in American Higher Education." In *Higher Education: Handbook of Theory and Research. Vol. II,* edited by John C. Smart, 43–84. New York: Agathon Press, 1986.

Index

access (library)
  defined, 108
  indicators of, 102–108, Figure 14
    (105)
access vs. ownership, 74, 77–81
agile organization (or library), 112
alumni support of libraries, 76, 89
American Library Association,
    founding, 4
Ashar, Hanna, 15, 38, 43, 96
ARL (Association of Research Li-
    braries) ranking, *see* reputa-
    tion and ranking of the li-
    brary

Bertanlanffy, Ludwig von, 26
bibliographic instruction, 9
bounded rationality, 24–25, 46
Boyer, Ernest L., 8
Brown, Richard H., 6
budgeting, defined, 31
budgets, 10, 75, 84

centrality (*see also* library centrality)
  defined, 36, 38–45, 77–81, 93,
    96
  immediacy, 36–38 (Figs. 4–6),

39–40, 48
  interconnectedness, 27, 28 (Fig.
    2), 40–48, 78–79, 96
  key concepts and uses, 2, 14, 15,
    17, 32–33, 35, 122
  mission congruence, 41–42, 48,
    78–79, 96
  pervasiveness, 36–38 (Figs.4–6),
    48, 139
  problems in definitions, 45–46,
    110–111
centrality index, 44
coalitions or coalition-building, 25,
    27, 28 (Fig. 2), 46, 48
College: The Undergraduate Experi-
    ence (Ernest L. Boyer), 8
connectedness, *see* centrality
contingency theory, *see* organization
    theory
coping with uncertainty, 35–38
    (Figs. 4–6), 48 (*see also* cen-
    trality and power)
criticality, *see* immediacy
crossroads community, *see* "the li-
    brary as crossroads commu-
    nity" metaphor
Crozier, Michel, 35–36

Cyert, R. M., 25
decision-making
    in organizations, 25 (Fig. 1), 27
        (Fig. 2), 46
    in universities, 11

Downs, Robert B., 12
departmental power, 15, 56–57 (*see
    also* power, subunit)

The Economics of Research Libraries
    (Martin Cummings), 10
Eliot, Charles William, 4
empirical indicators
    defined, 57–58, Appendix B
    discussed, 96–97
    related to library centrality,
        102–104, 105 (Fig. 13),
        110 (Fig. 16), 116 (Fig.
        18), Appendix B
environments, effects on organiza-
    tions, 24–25, 27, Figs.1–6,
    46
equifinality, 26–27, 46

faculty
    opinions of academic libraries,
        85–90, 113
    perceptions/views of academic li-
        braries, 8
    status or rank, 9, 92, 98–100
funding in academic libraries, *see*
    budgets

gap between instruction and the li-
    brary, 7
gateway to information metaphor,
    see "The library is the gate-
    way to information" meta-
    phor

geographic uniqueness of libraries,
    90
German university model, 3
grounded theory methodology, 56,
    96–97

Hackman, Judith Dozier, 38, 42,
    56–57, 96
Hardesty, Larry L., 8, 13, 57, 71
Hatch Act of 1887, 3
"heart of the university" metaphor,
    see "The library is the heart
    of the university" metaphor
Heath, Fred, 37, 112, 114
Hickson, D. J., et al., 35–38, 39
Hinings, C. A., et al., 35–38, 39

immediacy, 36–38 (Figs. 4–6), 39–
    40, 48 (*see also* centrality and
    library centrality)
information commons, 113–114,
    121
interrelatedness, *see* centrality
interview questions used in research
    study, 72–90, Appendix A
interviewees, description, 72, 73
    (Table 2)

Kaser, David, 13, 57, 71

"laundry list" of possible indicators
    of library centrality, 58–59,
    86 (Fig. 8)
librarians, attitudes and responsive-
    ness, 79, 91
Library Bureau, 4
library centrality (*see also* service,
    access, tradition, user success)
    defined, 16, 23, 48, 96, 100–115,
        101 (Fig. 10), 103 (Fig. 11),

104 (Fig. 12), 115*
empirical indicators, 102–104,
   105 (Fig. 13), 110 (Fig. 16),
   116 (Fig. 18), Appendix B
key concepts, 23
"laundry list" of possible indicators, 58–59, 86 (Fig. 8)
indicators, 15–16
non-indicators, 88–89, 96–100,
   97 (Fig. 9)
operational definition, 111–115,
   112 (Fig. 17), 115*
related to university teaching and
   research, 81–93
Library Journal, 4
library school closings, 33–34
Lyman, Peter, 118

Machiavelli, 24
March, James G., 25
McAnally, Arthur M., 12
metaphors
   uses in sociology, 6–7, 117–120
   "The library is the gateway to in-
      formation" metaphor, 117–
      118
   "The library is the heart of the
      university" metaphor, 1, 3–
      6, 14, 16–17, 72–77, 92,
      115–117
   "the library as crossroads commu-
      nity" metaphor, 115–122
   "The network is the library" meta-
      phor, 118
Moffett, William A., 6
Morrill Acts of 1861 and 1890, 3
Munn, Robert E., 12–13

National Information Infrastructure
   (NII), 7

negotiation, *see* coalitions and coalition-building

operational definition, defined, 58
organization theory (*see also*
   power)
   bounded rationality, 24–25, 46
   classical school, 24
   coalition-building, 25, 27, 28
      (Fig. 2), 46, 48
   contemporary school, 26, 46
   contingency school, 26–28
   decision-making, 11, 25 (Fig. 1),
      27 (Fig. 2)
   defined, 14
   environments, effects on organi-
      zations, 24–25 (Figs. 1–2, 6),
      27, 46
   equifinality, 26–27, 46
   history, 24–29, 46, 47 (Figs. 1–
      6)
   neoclassical school, 24–25 (Fig. 1)
   open systems, 27
   power/politics school, 27–29, 46–
      47, 113
   strategic contingencies theory,
      35–38;
      Crozier, 35–36
      components: coping with un-
         certainty, 35–38 (Figs. 4–6),
         48; substitutability, 35–48
         (Figs. 4–6), 48; centrality,
         35–48 (Figs. 4–6), 48 (*see also*
         centrality and library central-
         ity)
      Hickson et al., 35–36
      Hinings et al., 37
   systems school, 26–27
organizations
   as equilibrium systems, 25

dynamic quality, 24, 25 (Fig. 1), 28 (Fig. 2), 46

Parsons, Talcott, 25
peripheral units (of organizations), 42–43
Perrow, Charles, 35
pervasiveness, 36–38 (Figs. 4–6), 48, 139 (*see also* centrality and library centrality)
Pfeffer, Jeffrey, 56–57
pilot study, 66–67
power
    defined, 38
    reducing uncertainty, 35
    subunit, 15, 30, 34–38 (Figs. 3–6), 48 (*see also* departmental power)
practical role of the library, 76–77
Public Libraries in the United States: Their History, Condition, and Management, 4

reallocation, *see* resource allocation
reputation and ranking of the library, 26, 86–87, 91
research libraries, history, 3
resource allocation
    defined, 31–32
    studies, 15, 31–33, 56–57
retrenchment
    defined, 33
    studies, 15, 33–34
Rules for a Printed Catalog, 4

Salancik, Gerald R., 56–57
service (library)
    defined, 108
    discussed, 102–108, 105 (Fig. 14)

Simon, Herbert A., 24–25
students' opinions of academic libraries, 85–90, 91, 113
study hall, library used as, 8, 76, 79, 83–84, 85, 113, 116
"Standards for University Libraries" (ACRL), 2, 17, 39, 114
substitutability, 35–38 (Figs. 4–6), 48 (*see also* organization theory)
symbolic role of the academic library, 5, 13, 74–77, 87, 92, 96, 109

teaching library, 114, 121
Tompkins, Philip, 121
Total Quality Management (TQM), 112–113
tradition (library)
    defined, 108
    discussed, 108–110, 109 (Fig. 15)
transaction log analyses, 115
Tzu, Sun, 24

uncertainty, coping with, 35–38 (Figs. 4–6), 48 (*see also* centrality and power)
universities
    as organizations, characteristics, 29–31
    as organized anarchies, 30, 48
    mission (teaching, research, service), 81–85
    program review criteria, 33–34
universities participating in the research study, descriptions, 59–64, 65 (Table 1)
user success
    defined, 111–115
    discussed, 16, 111–115, 122
    schematic, 112 (Fig. 17)

surveys, 115
vs. user satisfaction, 112

value congruence, *see* mission congruence
Veaner, Allen B., 11

virtual library, 118, 121–122

Weiner, Norbert, 26
White, Herbert S., 13, 114
workflow pervasiveness, 36–37, 39, 43, 44 (*see also* centrality)